Mathematical Development in Young Children

EXPLORING NOTATIONS

Bárbara M. Brizuela

Foreword by Richard Lehrer

TEACHERS
COLLEGE
PRESS

Teachers College, Columbia University
New York and London

Published by Teachers College Press, 1234 Amsterdam Avenue, New York, NY 10027

Copyright © 2004 by Teachers College, Columbia University

Library of Congress Cataloging-in-Publication Data

Brizuela, Bárbara M.
   Mathematical development in young children : exploring notations / Bárbara M. Brizuela; foreword by Richard Lehrer.
      p.   cm. — (Ways of knowing in science and mathematics series)
   Includes bibliographical references and index.
   ISBN 0-8077-4452-2 (acid-free paper) — ISBN 0-8077-4451-4 (pbk. : acid-free paper)
      1. Mathematical notation.   2. Mathematics—Study and teaching (Elementary)   I. Title. II. Series.

   QA41.B75   2004
   372.7—dc22   2003068690

ISBN 0-8077-4451-4 (paper)
ISBN 0-8077-4452-2 (cloth)

Printed on acid-free paper
Manufactured in the United States of America

11   10   09   08   07   06   05   04   8   7   6   5   4   3   2   1

Ways of Knowing in Science and Mathematics Series

RICHARD DUSCHL, SERIES EDITOR

ADVISORY BOARD: Charles W. Anderson, Raffaella Borasi, Nancy Brickhouse, Marvin Druger, Eleanor Duckworth, Peter Fensham, William Kyle, Roy Pea, Edward Silver, Russell Yeany

Contents

Foreword

When we think of mathematics, images of doing often come to mind. Calculating sums and differences. Recalling key constructions. Finding solutions to equations. Images like these neglect the conceptual side of mathematics, the search for pattern and structure that motivates mathematical activity. MATHEMATICAL DEVELOPMENT IN YOUNG CHILDREN remedies a further oversight: Mathematical doing and conceiving are mediated by powerful and often complicated systems of writing, so mathematics is also a particular kind of written discourse. When we do mathematics, we participate in a rich tradition of symbolization, so commonplace that, as in other realms of the everyday, we fail to appreciate its extraordinary virtues. By taking a child's-eye view of mathematical symbolization, Bárbara Brizuela invites us to re-discover and appreciate anew the remarkable power and intellectual excitement of writing mathematics. In the hands of the children portrayed in this volume, these symbolic systems are not the relics of an age long past, but rather tools for discovering and exploring emerging worlds of number and pattern.

The approach taken is that of case study and clinical interview. By conversing with children as they write mathematics, the author reveals how her conversational partners are inventing and revising symbols to make, and make sense of, mathematics. We are first introduced to 5-year-old George, who signifies the quantity *seventeen* as 70 and the quantity *eighteen* as 08. Barbara's conversation with George reveals not madness but method, and as she traces the evolution of George's thinking, we are reminded anew of the complexity of our positional notation system for quantity. With George, we once again experience the role of position in distinguishing between quantities represented numerically ("place value") and the special status of zero. We come to see George not as mistaken, but as attempting to appropriate a powerful system to make sense of quantities. We find that he is experimenting with zero as a symbol that functions as a placeholder, although he is uncertain about its status or just how the base 10 system of numeration should be coordinated with position and numerals to represent any quantity. Yet his explorations are not undirected or uninfluenced by conventions, and they come into sharper focus as he attempts to create symbolizations that allow him to compare quantities. This dance between invention and cultural capital (e.g., children's familiarity with numerals and writing systems) comes into sharper relief in the next two chapters of the book. First, we meet Paula, another kindergartner. Paula interprets two-digit numerals by drawing an analogy to other forms of writing: 4 in 46 denotes *forty* and not *four* because its position indicates a "capital number." For Paula, positional notation is sensible by analogy to words. The role of a word is signaled by capitalization and the role of a numeral by position. What is sensible to Paula is a syntax, not mere punctuation, so she employs what she knows about one system to re-create another. The interplay and mutual support between invention and convention is further exemplified by Thomas, a 6-year-old child who appropriates other pieces of linguistic punctuation, periods and commas, to appreciate their roles in writing numbers at the edge of imagination.

These cases of co-origination and development of early number concepts and writing are elaborated and extended to new mathematical realms in the remainder of the volume. In work the author conducted with her colleagues Analúcia Schliemann and David Carraher, readers are introduced to children who are making sense of fractions, data tables, and Cartesian coordinates. Sara, a third grader, represents fractions to help structure her thinking about the actions represented in word problems, and even uses her representations to re-structure her thinking, so that the notations help her see what is alike and different about quantities across different problems. Along the way, we come to see that Sara is developing meta-representational competence as she reasons about how particular symbolic expressions help, or fail to help, support her efforts to solve problems. Sara's efforts are complemented by those of peers who are constructing tables to represent changes in quantities. By inventing their own tables, children come to see the mathematical work performed by conventional tables, and we again are provided a glimpse of children constructing symbolic systems that they see as purposeful and fruitful. The theme of meta-representational competence flowers in the penultimate chapter of this volume as children coordinate multiple notational systems to reason simultaneously about two linear functions. This chapter also illuminates how even when children appropriate symbolic schemes invented by their classmates, they nonetheless re-purpose them to their own ends. Notations compress meanings and allow individuals to assess their own understandings, and they also allow understandings to be shared between individuals via a common index. The concluding chapter reiterates and amplifies the themes so amply illustrated in the preceding chapters. We find ourselves reminded of what was once problematic and inspired to support anew children's mathematical development.

Richard Lehrer
Vanderbilt University

Acknowledgments

The work reflected in this book merits two kinds of acknowledgments: a chapter-by-chapter recognition of the contributions and support provided, and a more general thanks.

Chapter 2 of this book was developed as part of my doctoral dissertation at the Harvard Graduate School of Education (HGSE). I am grateful to Eleanor Duckworth and Claryce Evans (HGSE), Analúcia Schliemann (Tufts University) and Emilia Ferreiro (DIE, CINVESTAV, Mexico) for their support and feedback during the study's inception, development, and analysis. Jeanne Bamberger (MIT) also participated in some of the discussions related to this study and contributed in important ways to my thinking about notations of social use. The Spencer Foundation's Research Training Grant Program at HGSE provided me financial support during most of this study's development. Kitty Boles (HGSE) supported my work as a Spencer liaison at HGSE. My visit in the spring of 1998 to Emilia Ferreiro and her research group in Mexico was pivotal for the theoretical framing of the research reported in this chapter.

The research developed for Chapter 3 was carried out under the guidance of Analúcia Schliemann, to whom I am deeply grateful. Parts of this chapter have been previously published in the international journal *For the Learning of Mathematics*.

The research reported in Chapter 4 benefited from comments and discussions with those involved in the HGSE course T150, Curriculum Based on Understanding, in the spring of 1998. Besides the support from my peers, I also benefited from feedback from Eleanor Duckworth, Fiona Hughes-McDonnell, and Isabella Knox.

The data from Chapters 5, 6, and 7 come from the TERC/Tufts University Early Algebra study, directed by David Carraher (TERC) and Analúcia Schliemann (Tufts University). Funding for this project has been provided by the National Science Foundation through grants #9722732 and #9909591, awarded to Analúcia Schliemann and David Carraher.

Chapter 5 is based on previous presentations by myself, David Carraher, and Analúcia Schliemann at the Research Presession, 2000 meeting of the NCTM, Chicago, and at the Ninth International Congress of Mathematical Education (ICME), Tokyo-Makuhari, Japan, in August 2000. Special thanks to Pat Thompson (Vanderbilt University) and Susanna Lara-Roth (Tufts University) for constructive comments on earlier versions of this chapter.

The original version of Chapter 6 was coauthored with Susanna Lara-Roth (Tufts University). This chapter was originally presented at the meeting of the International Conference for Mathematics Instruction (ICMI) in Australia in December 2001, and a version of this chapter was previously published in the *Journal of Mathematical Behavior*.

Chapter 7 benefited from the help of Susanna Lara-Roth and Jerry Karacz, who assisted with videotaping and camerawork during the interview. My thanks also to Tracy Noble (TERC/Tufts University) for her orientation regarding the "gestures" literature.

In more general terms, my first thanks go to the countless children who have helped to shape my thinking and reflecting about mathematical notations. Specifically, I thank the children presented in this book: George, Paula, Thomas, and the second and third graders who formed part of the Early Algebra research project from fall 1998 to spring 2001. Thanks also go to their parents, teachers, and school principals, who graciously let me into their homes, classrooms, and schools.

Analúcia Schliemann and David Carraher have supported my work, by providing enormous encouragement, space, and opportunities to continue to pursue my interests in children's mathematical notations in the Early Algebra project, and by taking my interests seriously. Thanks also to other members of the Early Algebra project: Darrell Earnest, Anne Goodrow, Susanna Lara-Roth, and Irit Peled.

The work of Emilia Ferreiro has profoundly influenced my research. Her research, with a rigor and depth of analysis that I continue to strive for, is a model for me. Her knowledge of the literature and research and her keen eye for analysis and research have proved invaluable during the process of writing this book. Emilia graciously encouraged me to join her seminars in Mexico during two periods—for 2 months in January–February 1998, and for 2 weeks in March 2000. I am very grateful to have had these opportunities and to have shared discussions with such a great mind and with some of her students. My interactions with Celia Díaz, Celia Zamudio, Mónica Alvarado, Graciela Quinteros, and Mirta Castedo were especially important.

Eleanor Duckworth's approach to clinical interviewing also has had a great impact on my approach to research and to interviewing children. Her subtle ways of approaching interviews with children were a feast to watch in T440 at HGSE. The thorough nature of her interviewing and her vision of the capacity of children's minds are other goals that I strive for.

My conversations and interactions with Mónica Alvarado, Jim Kaput, Richard Lehrer, Delia Lerner, Eduardo Martí, Luis Moreno Armella, and Nora Scheuer, all interested in the area of mathematical representations and notations, have been very fruitful and helpful. Rachel Kramer and Angelita Collins provided great help in putting together this manuscript.

Many thanks also to my countless friends and special people in my life who have given me love, support, and stimulation during the last few years.

And last but not least, to Pablo, Azul, and Sofía. Thank you for your patience, understanding, love, and support.

Mathematical Development in Young Children

Overview

Interest in mathematical notations has increased significantly over the past few years (see, for example, Cobb, Yackel, & McClain, 2000; Gravemeijer, Lehrer, van Oers, & Verschaffel, 2002). This interest can be seen, for example, in recent standards and principles put forth by the National Council of Teachers of Mathematics (NCTM), which include representations as one of the process standards to be met across grades, from prekindergarten through Grade 12 (NCTM, 2000). Additionally, NCTM's 2001 yearbook was devoted to different aspects of mathematical notations (Cuoco & Curcio, 2001). Notations, understood simultaneously as the act of representing and the object itself, are central to learners' mathematical development and to the development of the mathematical discipline. In fact, notations are an essential aspect of mathematics learning and teaching (Cuoco & Curcio, 2001).

Young children of diverse socioeconomic and cultural contexts are immersed in a world of mathematical notations from the time they come into the world. Written numbers that surround them represent a large variety of numerical and quantitative concepts, as well as being used for other, different purposes (e.g., as labels and in telephone numbers; see Sinclair & Sinclair, 1984). The same degree of exposure is true of other mathematical notations (e.g., Lehrer, Schauble, Carpenter, & Penner, 2000) such as graphs and tables (e.g., diSessa, Hammer, Sherin, & Kolpakowski, 1991) and notations for space and measurement (e.g., Lehrer et al., 2000), for example.

However, in spite of these efforts, Ferreiro (1996a) has pointed out, "in the domain of notations of social use, our knowledge of the psychogenesis of mathematical notation is still rather poor" (p. 138). In this book I address this gap in the research. Doing so is important not only in order to answer significant research questions but also in terms of teaching practice. In spite of the fact that recent standards and principles put forth by researchers and NCTM push for the inclusion of mathematical notations as an integral part of the teaching and learning of mathematics, to date most teachers have received little or no training in the area. Researchers have recognized the importance of notations in mathematics education, but these reflections and observations have not yet had an impact on in-service or preservice teacher education.

The research reported in this book connects very closely to an important line of inquiry spearheaded by Emilia Ferreiro (e.g., Ferreiro & Teberosky, 1979) regarding children's learning of written language. For more than 20 years, in her work Ferreiro has viewed written language as a conceptual object—a position I also take: seeing mathematical notations as conceptual objects. By *conceptual object* I mean things (such as notations) about which children think, develop ideas, and reflect. With Ferreiro, I assume that written systems constitute conceptual objects. That is, children's learning of mathematical notations is not merely a matter of perceptive-motor skills. Although Ferreiro's research has been carried out in the area of written language, I share many of the assumptions underlying her research. For example, I assume that there exists both a socially constituted object with certain characteristics and a logic that characterizes it and, on the part of the child, hypotheses regarding mathematical notation systems and how they work. In appropriating systems of notations, children are trying to understand the relationships between the elements of the system and the way the system works (Ferreiro, 1991). Additionally, I posit that children reconstruct social notation systems and that the ideas they develop are constitutive of the conventional ideas they will later develop (Ferreiro, 1991).

There are other assumptions underlying this book. First, with Ferreiro (1991), I believe that conventional knowledge is built on prior understandings. From this perspective, it follows that young children's ideas about mathematical notations could be constitutive of their later conventional understandings about more complex kinds of notations and about mathematics in general. Additionally, with Sinclair (1988), I assume that children's ideas prior to their conventional understanding of mathematical notations make sense within the context of their own view of mathematics, although they might seem naive or "senseless" to adults.

Moreover, Ferreiro's research is deeply grounded in Piaget's conception of the child as a knowing subject who creates and transforms in order to learn and understand. This concept underlies both Ferreiro's work and this book. From this perspective, the child who is trying to understand and learn mathematical notations does not merely receive or copy the information that he or she receives from her or his milieu. On the contrary, there is an active and complex effort on the part of the child to construct her or his own understandings and interpretations. Thus, both Piaget and Ferreiro's work constitute part of the theoretical underpinnings of this book.

RESEARCH FOCUS

Research in developmental psychology has documented children's developing number sense (e.g., Cobb & Wheatly, 1988; Dehaene, 1997; Fuson, 1988; Hughes, 1986; Kamii, 1985, 1989, 2000; Steffe & Cobb, 1988). During their first years of life and then of their schooling, children develop understandings about numbers and how they relate to quantities, about how numbers can be decomposed into ones and tens, about the ordinal and cardinal properties of numbers, and about what happens when you add or subtract numbers. As children develop number sense, they also develop ways to represent that number sense and gradually appropriate conventional notation systems used in their daily world.

Tolchinsky and Karmiloff-Smith (1992) have distinguished between two perspectives in the study of notations: that of studying notations and what they represent and that of studying the notations themselves. They call the first perspective "notations as referential-communicative tools" and the second "notations as domains of knowledge" (p. 287. Regarding what notations "refer" to, I believe that they always refer to something, i.e., they always have some meaning for a person—however hidden from the outsider).

Two examples might clarify the difference between *notations as referential-communicative tools* and *notations as domains of knowledge*. Sinclair's study (1988) exemplifies the first perspective, that of *notations as referential-communicative tools*. Sinclair presented children with collections of objects and asked them to show with notations how many objects there were. She thus centered on the relationship between children's notations and the quantities they represent. In contrast, Lerner and Sadovsky (1994) studied children's numerical *notations as a domain of knowledge*. They concentrated on written numbers, asking children to make comparisons without necessarily referring to external collections of objects. For instance, they asked children to play the card game of War, in which children placed cards on the table and whoever had the card with the greatest number got to keep all the cards. Whoever ended up with most cards won the game. The cards that they presented to the children had only written numbers between 5 and 31 on them—with no drawings. In this book, I will be focusing on both perspectives—what notations refer to and notations as conceptual objects or domains of knowledge. The types of notations I will focus on in this book are notations for the number system (including, among other aspects, place value and the use of punctuation marks in numbers), fractions, data tables, graphs, vectors, number lines, and natural language.

Previous research exploring young children's written mathematical notations has focused on the differentiations children make between notations for language and for number (Tolchinsky & Karmiloff-Smith, 1992) and on the progression in the types of notations children use when they represent quantities (e.g., Hughes, 1986; Sastre & Moreno, 1976; Sinclair, 1988). This research has explored the connections between children's notations and their ideas about place value (e.g., Bednarz & Janvier, 1982; Bergeron, Herscovics, & Sinclair, 1992; Kamii, 1985, 2000; Kamii, 1982; Ross, 1986). There have also been explorations of children's notations for space and measurement (e.g., Lehrer et al., 2000), graphs (e.g., diSessa et al., 1991), arithmetical operations (e.g., Fuson, 1986; Hughes, 1986; Kamii, 1985, 1989, 2000; Willis & Fuson, 1988), arithmetic problem solving (e.g., Carpenter, Ansell, Franke, Fennema, & Weisbeck, 1993; Hiebert et al., 1996), and data (e.g., Lehrer & Schauble, 2002; Tierney & Nemirovsky, 1995). In addition, there have been explorations of older students' mathematical notations (e.g., Confrey, 1991).

The work of Sastre and Moreno (1976), Sinclair (1988), and Hughes (1986) explores the progression in the types of notations children use when they make notations for quantities. Each of these studies are attempts to describe the spontaneous notations children make when shown different quantities of objects, and the authors report similar findings. In general, they identify a progression in children's notations that only gradually includes the use of written numbers in a conventional way. Children begin by using idiosyncratic marks and later are able to establish a one-to-one correspondence between their notations and the quantity of objects represented, using one graphism for each object being represented. Some children use letters, some use numbers, while others use letters and numbers in their one-to-one correspondences with objects. The use of letters when representing quantity reflects a lack of differentiation between letters and numbers. Further, some children use the same graphic mark throughout, aligning identical shapes for one display (e.g., OOOO), while others use the stock of shapes they know to make varied sequences (e.g., oσ∂∩). The use of the same mark throughout versus a variation of marks is an interesting approach in light of previous research that shows that in the area of written language children develop a hypothesis wherein strings of the same letters are not considered as words (Ferreiro & Teberosky, 1979). Thus, the acceptance of the use of the same graphism to represent amount, and its rejection to represent written language, reflects the fact that children make an important distinction between written language and written number (Tolchinsky, 1993). As they get older, children begin to limit themselves to the use of written numbers in their notations. A few write down the sequence corresponding to the number of objects (e.g., 1234), and others write the number the amount of times that is correct according to one-to-one correspondence (e.g., 4444). Finally, children will write the number corresponding to the number of objects being represented, accompanied by the name of the object (e.g., 4 ducks).

Tolchinsky and Karmiloff-Smith (1992) explore how children decide which combinations of elements belong to "writing" and "counting" and which do not belong to "writing" and to "counting." What they ask themselves is what constraints children employ for numbers to be numbers, for letters to be letters, and for words to be words. They give children a set of cards with various notations printed on them, and ask them which of the cards are "not good for writing" (p. 291) and which cards are not good for counting. Their study shows that very young children do not confuse written language and numbers and that these children put in place different constraints for deciding which notation is which.

In their research, Bednarz and Janvier (1982); Bergeron et al. (1992); C. Kamii (1985); M. Kamii (1982); and Ross (1986) have explored children's place value notation. These scholars explore the meaning that different digits in multidigit numbers have for children. For example, the child is presented with a collection of discrete objects and the corresponding two-digit number, or with a collection of discrete objects and the request to produce a notation to show how many objects there are. The child is asked how each separate digit in the notation corresponds to items in the collection. In general terms, this research shows that children find it difficult to think of the digit in the tens place of a number as representing the number of sets of 10 objects; instead, children might say that the 2 in 24 refers to two objects in the collection.

An important aspect of this book relates to what Goldin and Shteingold (2001) have referred to as the "representational perspective." This perspective

> involves explicit focus on both the external and the internal, with the utmost attention given to the interplay between them. Through interaction with structured external representations in the learning environment, students' internal representation systems develop. The students can then generate new external representations. (p. 8)

Other research (e.g., diSessa et al., 1991; Lehrer & Schauble, 2000; Lehrer et al., 2000) has also shown the fruitfulness of contrasting spontaneous and conventional notations.

Few educators would contest the need to take into account students' mathematical notations. However, what does this mean for the actual practice of mathematics education? What sorts of notations do young students typically make in mathematics? How do students' notations evolve over time? How do they compare to conventions being introduced in school?

When can children's spontaneous notations serve as bridges to conventional symbolic notations? When are they best left by the wayside, substituted, ultimately, by more promising notations? These are some of the questions that will be addressed throughout this book.

The data collected for this volume relied heavily on the use of Piagetian clinical interviews (see Piaget, 1926/1976), with a due influence from the work of Eleanor Duckworth (1996). The interviews took place both in and out of classrooms; they were both individual and group interviews. According to Piaget, the clinical interview is

> experimental in the sense that the practitioner sets himself a problem, makes hypotheses, adapts the conditions to them and finally controls each hypothesis by testing it against the reactions he stimulates in conversation. . . . The clinical examination is also dependent on direct observation, in the sense that the good practitioner lets himself be led, though always in control, and takes account of the whole of the mental context. (1926/1976, p. 8)

In the clinical interview, the interviewer must know how to observe, "that is to say, to let the child talk freely" (p. 9).

Duckworth's (1996) work has influenced the way in which the interviews were carried out in that they are both "extended" over time and carried out, at times, in group settings. In addition, her approach to the presentation of opportunities for interviewees to explore the subject matter to its fullest has had an impact on the work described in this book. As she herself puts it, in the clinical interview, the researcher/teacher

> must provide some accessible entry points, must present the subject matter from different angles, elicit different responses from different learners, open a variety of paths for exploration, engender conflicts, and provide surprises, . . . encourage learners to open out beyond themselves, and help them realize that there are other points of view yet to be uncovered—that they have not yet exhausted the thoughts they might have about this matter. (pp. 135–136)

In addition, readers of this book will notice the influence of Inhelder, Sinclair, and Bovet's work (1974), in the way in which conflicting situations are presented to children, and in that their ideas and thinking are followed over time, their "cognitive acquisitions . . . and transition processes" examined (p. 17).

CONNECTIONS TO HISTORY OF MATHEMATICS AND NOTATIONAL SYSTEMS

Throughout this book, connections will be made to both the history of mathematics and the history of notational systems in different fields, such as music, written language, and mathematics. Through the connections that are established, I will try to develop more thorough understandings of the types of mechanisms of thought and cognitive obstacles that can be identified in the development of mathematical notations, as well as the similarities between the mechanisms and obstacles observed in children's development and throughout history (see Ferreiro, 1991; Ferreiro & Teberosky, 1979). The history of mathematical notations can help to shed light on developing understandings about children's notations for problems (see Ferreiro, Pontecorvo, & Zucchermaglio, 1996). The connections and similarities, however, are not intended to provide a causal connection or an ontogenesis-follows-or-repeats-phylogenesis perspective. On the contrary, I share the assumption of Ferreiro and her colleagues (Ferreiro, Pontecorvo, & Zucchermaglio, 1996) that exploring the history of a discipline can help in constructing understandings about children's development. Their explanation for the inclusion of historical data in the context of the study of children's literacy development is of interest:

> This historical digression is not aimed at supporting a hypothesis of parallelism between the psychogenetic and ontogenetic development of writing. . . . It is possible, however, that during the acquisition of written language the child is faced with some fundamental problems that were present in the historical development of written languages. (p. 149)

The types of cognitive obstacles and approximations to written numbers that can be identified throughout history can help us understand children's own attempts to represent the same concepts. Furthermore, the articulation of the study of children's development and the development of the practices studied throughout history can help us to develop a more complex and accurate understanding of children's development in various areas.

A DEFINITION FOR NOTATIONS

Establishing a definition of what is meant in this book by *notations* is important. I will be focusing on what Martí and Pozo (2000) have called "external systems of representation," to differentiate these from mental representations. Thus, in this book, I will be focusing mostly on external representations, made with pencil and paper and having a physical existence. Goldin also refers to "external representations" (1998; Goldin & Shteingold, 2001) to distinguish them from internal representations. These external representations are "the shared, somewhat standardized representational systems developed through human social processes" (Goldin,

1998, p. 146). My definition of mathematical notations borrows from Goldin, Hughes, Kaput, Lehrer, and Martí. They relate to what Lehrer and Schauble (2000) call "representational models": material inscriptions that sometimes form part of representation systems, but that can also be nonconventional and nonsystematic. Using Kaput's (1991) words, representation systems are the "materially realizable cultural or linguistic artifacts shared by a cultural or language community" (p. 55). Hughes (1986) also refers to these kinds of representations as "symbolic" representations: those representations that correspond to widely adopted conventions.

With these caveats in mind, however, it is important to make a further distinction between notations and representations. In keeping with an understanding of representations as internal, or mental (see Freeman, 1993), Lee and Karmiloff-Smith (1996) have distinguished between notations and representations in the following way:

> We reserve the term "representation" to refer to what is internal to the mind and the term "notation" to what is external to the mind. . . . While representation reflects how knowledge is constructed in the mind, notation establishes a "stand for" relationship between a referent and a sign. (p. 127)

Lee and Karmiloff-Smith (1996) argue that external representations include writing, numerical notations, drawings, maps, and any other form of graphic marks created intentionally. These kinds of external representations are characterized by having an existence independent of their creator, having a material existence that guarantees their permanence, and constituting organized systems. According to Martí and Pozo (2000), in order for an entity to be considered a system, there must be at least a relationship between a graphic mark and what it represents. Following this definition, almost any notation can be considered as part of a system. Nemirovsky's (1994) definition of what counts as a symbol system is helpful in clarifying what is meant by *system*:

> With "symbol system" I refer to the analysis of mathematical representations in terms of rules. For example, Cartesian graphs can be considered as a symbol system; that is, a rule-governed set of elements, such as points being determined by coordinate values in specific ways on scales demarking units regularly. (p. 390)

Given the variations in the definitions of representation, I have chosen to use the term *notation* throughout this book. Thus, notations fall under what some researchers have called external representations. Furthermore, the inevitable relationships or rules established by creators of notations between their graphic marks and what they intend to represent, lead these notations, be they idiosyncratic or conventional, to form part of larger notation systems.

ORGANIZATION OF THE BOOK

This volume is organized chronologically in terms of the ages of the children described in each of the chapters. This leads to two overlapping sequences: an order in terms of increasing age of the children (5 through 9 years of age), and an order in terms of the increasing complexity of the mathematical content dealt with in the notations. I have used pseudonyms to protect the privacy of the children I have studied. In Chapters 3, 5, 6, and 7, I use children's real first names, at children's and parents' request or with their permission.

In Chapter 2, I focus on George, a 5-year-old kindergarten student who will be presented trying to create a systematic way of writing numbers, in his own idiosyncratic way, and trying to understand how the written number system works. Specifically, I will focus on George's way of writing "teens," and how this might relate to his developing understandings about the written number system and about place value.

In Chapter 3, my focus is Paula, another 5-year-old kindergarten student who, in the process of developing a system for naming and writing two-digit numbers beyond 12, invents the idea of "capital numbers." The interaction between inventions and conventions, one of the main issues presented in this book, will be highlighted in Paula's chapter.

Thomas is the focus of Chapter 4. Thomas is a very sophisticated 6-year-old kindergarten student who, during a series of extended clinical interviews, deals with the role and function of commas and periods in numbers. His case highlights the connections between children's ideas and the history of mathematical notations, as well as the gradually evolving conceptual understandings about the written number system and the notations used to represent those evolving understandings.

The data in Chapters 5, 6, and 7 come from the Early Algebra project, directed by Analúcia Schliemann (Tufts University) and David Carraher (TERC). Sara is the central topic in Chapter 5. Sara is a third grader who will be shown developing notations for problems dealing with fractions. The focus of the chapter will be not only her evolving understanding of the problems, fractions, and their notations, but also her use of the notations to "help her think," as she explains it herself. The events that will be analyzed in Chapter 5 come from classroom events in which she discusses the most appropriate type of notation with her friends, and from a follow-up in a subsequent clinical interview.

In Chapter 6, we move into even more complex mathematics, while remaining in the K–3 focus of the book. This chapter contains descriptions of the work with data tables of a group of second and third graders, with an emphasis on Jennifer, one of these children. Through describing Jennifer's work with data tables, I will highlight the evolution of her thinking about mathematical concepts such as additive relations, her ideas about data tables in general, and the ways in which children bring into notations, such as data tables, their own idiosyncratic methods of representation as well as the conventions that they gradually appropriate.

In Chapter 7, I explore the interrelations of different types of notations. This chapter focuses on an extended clinical interview that I carried out with three third graders—Jennifer, Nathan, and Jeffrey—in which we explored a problem dealing with functions and sought different ways to represent the problem. During the interview, the children examined different types of notations: data tables, number lines, graphs, and natural language. This chapter will bring together many of the points that were raised in previous chapters: the ways in which the children used the notations to help them think through the problem; the ways in which they combined their own spontaneous ways of representing and the conventions that they had already appropriated; and the ways in which the notations reflect and embody the conceptual understandings about functions that the children held.

In Chapter 8, I gather together some of the main ideas presented throughout the book, highlighting the learning process behind mathematical notations and the importance of Piaget's theory in our thinking about this field.

George: Written Numbers and the Written Number System

GEORGE: (Writing 70) Seventeen. There's the seven (pointing to 7) and there's the teen (pointing to zero).

BÁRBARA: And where is the teen here (pointing to his writing of 18 as 08)? Eighteen. Where is the teen?

GEORGE: This is the teen (pointing to the zero in 08).

Children's learning of written numbers involves learning not only the isolated elements of the system but also, simultaneously, learning about the system itself and the rules that govern the system. For example, children learn that our written number system is made up of a finite number of elements—10 digits, zero through 9—and that these digits are combined in infinite ways to compose the different numbers. They must also learn about the rules that govern the system, for example, about base 10 and place value, among other features. The focus of this chapter is George's ideas about written numbers and the way they work.

The written number system we use is represented through two main features: base 10 and place value. The base of the written number system means that a number of units in a given place is denoted by 1 in the next higher place. In base 10, therefore, 10 units in the units place are denoted by 1 in the next higher (10s) place. Historian Ifrah (1981/1985) believes that the base 10 was chosen because "it is anatomically convenient" (p. 34), because of our 10 fingers. Additionally, however, base 10 does have some advantages over large bases such as 20 and 60, because few number words are required and therefore the range of numbers is within our memory capacity. Base 10 also has advantages over smaller bases, such as 2 or 3, that are much less convenient in writing. Other bases, however, coexist with our base 10 number system. Base 60, for example, is used for measuring time, arcs, and angles (Ifrah, 1985; Struik, 1987). In French spoken numeration, base 20 coexists with base 10 (*quatre-vingts* [four 20s] is 80, and *quatre-vingt-dix* [four 20s and 10] is 90).

Place value is implied in the base 10 system. Because of the place value feature of our written number system, there is a geometric progression as you move from place to place in a written number (Confrey, 1994; Confrey & Smith, 1995; Lampert, 1989). Digits from zero to 9 are used, and these digits are combined in various ways to form written numbers; the value of the number is determined by the digits and the place that each of them occupies. Place value allows us to use a limited number of digits (10 digits in the sequence zero, 1, 2, 3, 4, 5, 6, 7, 8, 9) to record any integer, no matter how large or how small. The digit 1 written in the units position (to the immediate left of the decimal point or to the extreme right if there is no decimal point) denotes one unit; the same digit written in the place to the left of the units denotes ten; the same digit written in the position to the left of the tens place signifies one hundred; the next position one thousand, and so forth. Historians have called the place-value system "undoubtedly one of the most fertile inventions of humanity" (Neugebauer, 1962, p. 5)—making arithmetical operations relatively easy to perform and making the written number system a relatively easy one to understand. The concept of place value was developed for the first time by the mathematicians and astronomers of Babylon, probably at the beginning of the second millenium B.C. (Ifrah, 1985).

Another feature of our written number system is the use of zero to function as a placeholder. This use was introduced as early as 300 B.C. by the Babylonians. Babylonian mathematicians used zero in a medial position in numbers (as in the number 408), and astronomers used it in that position as well as in final and initial positions (as in 30 and in sexagesimal fractions). In the history of numerical notations, the introduction of the use of zero as a placeholder was very important in reducing ambiguity in the interpretation of written numbers (that is, if no zero were included in 30, how would we know that the number is 30 and not 3?). However, the *concept* of zero to indicate absence, as a number, existed among the Hindus of the 6th or 7th centuries, but there existed no *notation* for this concept. "There are early texts in which the word *nya,* meaning zero, is explicitly used" (Struik, 1987, p. 67). The notation of zero as we use it today—*both* to indicate the number zero *and* to function as a placeholder—seems to be a relatively recent invention (sometime after the 6th century but before the 12th).

The written number system we use allows for simplicity and an economical way of representing numbers. It also permits simple everyday and highly complex calculations to be performed. Base 10 and place value, however, have been only some among many other ways of recording numbers. Other number systems have used the base 10 without place value (the Chinese notational system is a particularly clear example); still others have used positional notation and bases other than 10 (the Babylonian system had both a sexagesimal and a decimal character).

By exploring young children's understanding of written numbers, we can unearth some of the hypotheses that children develop regarding how written numbers and the written number system work. Ferreiro (1986a) has used the term *hypothesis* to refer broadly to ideas or systems of ideas constructed by children to explain the nature and way of functioning of written language as an object of knowledge. I am using the word *hypothesis* with the same meaning. At times I will use the terms *ideas, systems of ideas,* or *hypotheses* in analogous ways. Similarly, Vergnaud (1985, 1988) has spoken about children's "theorems in action" and Karmiloff-Smith and Inhelder (1975) about children's "theories."

In this chapter, the example of George highlights some of the ideas developed by children as they appropriate written numbers. The case also highlights the kind of logic constructed by children regarding the written number system, a logic that parallels the logic that underlies the system itself.

George was a 5-year-old child who attended a public kindergarten. He was interviewed individually as part of a larger study involving 30 kindergarten children (Brizuela, 2001). George lived in an urban-rim community, and the families living in his neighborhood were lower/lower-middle-class, working-class families from a wide variety of racial and ethnic backgrounds.

During the interview, he was presented with a series of tasks in which his understanding of written numbers and the written number system were explored. He was asked, in the different tasks, to both interpret and produce written numbers.

GEORGE'S FINE-MOTOR SKILLS AND UNDERSTANDING OF THE NUMBER SYSTEM

During our interview, the graphic marks that George made were clumsy and imperfect. However, I will argue that his imperfect graphic marks are not good predictors of his understanding of the number system. That is, even though he manifested some difficulties in making the shapes for the written numbers, he had already developed some complex ideas regarding the logic underlying the written number system. Learning about written numbers, then, does *not* mean merely learning how to make the shapes and how to perfect perceptive-motor skills; it does not involve tasks such as filling out worksheets with dots to connect and pages with the correct shapes for each number.

In the following excerpt, George had already been asked to write numbers 7, 1, 9, 19, and 8 (see Figure 2.1). I then asked him several questions:

BÁRBARA: Which one is more? Of all the numbers here. One, seven, nine, eight (pointing to George's writing). Which one is more?

GEORGE: (Points to 9—his number 9 [see Figure 2.1c])

BÁRBARA: Nine? How do you know?

GEORGE: Easy, cause first you go to one, then you go to two, then you go to three, then you go to four, then you go to five, then you go to six, then you go to seven, then you go to eight, then you go to nine (writing each of these numbers as he names and counts it [Figure 2.2]).

BÁRBARA: Could you make ten?

GEORGE: A zero and a one (writes 01 [Figure 2.3]). Then you go to nine, no, ten.

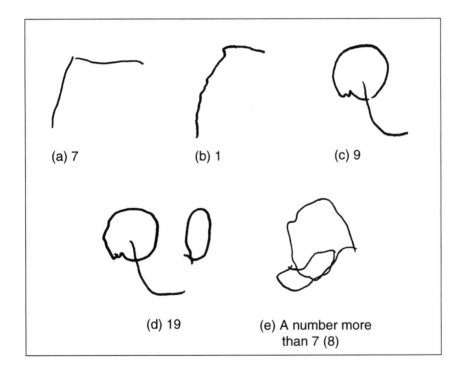

(a) 7   (b) 1   (c) 9

(d) 19   (e) A number more than 7 (8)

Figure 2.1. George's writing of several unordered numbers.

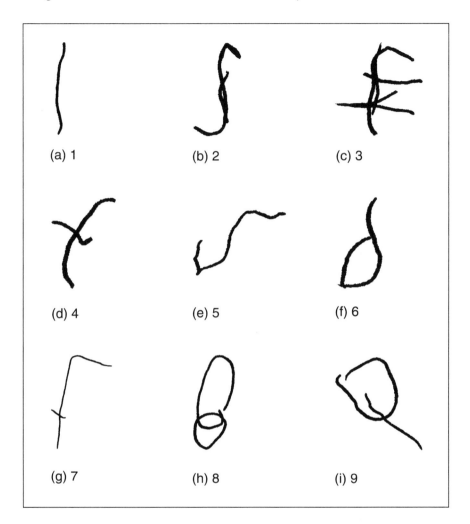

Figure 2.2. George's writing of 1 through 9.

In George's writing of the numbers 1 through 9, we can see that he has much difficulty in making the different shapes. In fact, many times it would have been very hard for me to distinguish what number he was writing, if I hadn't been paying close attention and hadn't been taking careful notes while he was working. However, as we will see below, his imperfect writing says nothing about the reflections that he had begun to make about the written number system. In a similar way, in the area of written language, researchers (e.g., Ferreiro & Teberosky, 1979) have highlighted that chil-

Figure 2.3. George's writing of 10.

dren's fine-motor skills and their imperfect writing say little about their complex understandings.

GEORGE'S USE OF DUMMY NUMBERS

The process of appropriating written numbers is not an automatic one. On the contrary, it is a constructive process, complex, full of ins and outs. Children interact with written numbers every day of their lives: on street signs, on doors, on telephones, on currency bills and coins, on TV. Slowly, they begin to construct an understanding about how the written number system works. In addition, they begin to associate the counting words with the written numbers associated with them: one-two-three-four-five-six-seven-eight-nine-ten . . . 1-2-3-4-5-6-7-8-9-10 . . .

In the process of beginning to write what for young children are more complex numbers, such as two-digit numbers, it makes sense to think that it takes them some time to learn how to write them. For instance, when I asked George to write the number 19, he said: "I don't know how to do that. But at least I will write a nine" (see Figure 2.4, left). Here George

Figure 2.4. George's writing of 9 and 19.

Figure 2.5. George's writing of 18.

indicated that 9 was an element of 19; by saying "at least," he was indicating that there might be an element missing in his writing.

> BÁRBARA: OK. So is the nine in nineteen? Is that one (pointing to the 9 he had written) in nineteen?
> GEORGE: Yeah.
> BÁRBARA: And what's it missing then? If it's to be nineteen?
> GEORGE: Teen (adding a zero to his writing in Figure 2.4 and ending up with 90 [see Figure 2.4, right]).

Later during the interview, I asked George to write the number 14.

> GEORGE: I'll make a small one. Small eighteen.
> BÁRBARA: Fourteen you're writing, or eighteen?
> GEORGE: (Writing 08 [Figure 2.5]) Eighteen.
> BÁRBARA: OK. You wrote eighteen. Could you write eighty-three?
> GEORGE: No, but I can write seventeen.
> BÁRBARA: Let's see, write seventeen.
> GEORGE: (Writing 70 [Figure 2.6]) Seventeen. There's the seven (pointing to 7) and there's the teen (pointing to zero).
> BÁRBARA: And where is the teen here (pointing to his writing of 18 [see Figure 2.5] as 08)? Eighteen. Where is the teen?
> GEORGE: This is the teen (pointing to the zero in 08).

In this exchange, there are important things that George shows us he knows and does not know. First of all, George never named zero as "zero"; he called it "teen." George clearly pointed to the symbol 0 as being the teen element of the number. He clearly stated at first that he did not know how to write teen and then decided to write zero for teen. He was also *aware*

Figure 2.6. George's writing of 17.

of the fact that he did not know some things about writing numbers. He knew that the number 9 was written and included in 19, 8 was written in 18, and 7 was written in 17. He also knew and was aware that there was another part of the number that he explicitly stated he did not know—the "teen." He said he did "not know how to [write the number 19]," stated that his writing was missing the teen, and subsequently wrote zero to stand for teen. He acknowledged that there was a part of the number that he did not know and finally decided to include the zero to stand in for this part. In the context of this interview, it is not clear and we cannot know if George was aware that the symbol he was using was actually zero; from the data gathered, we can simply assume that he was using a symbol to stand in for teen, but the connection with zero was not necessarily there for George. Alvarado and Ferreiro (2000; see also Alvarado, 2002) have reported the same type of reaction in 5-year-old Mexican children. They have called this type of solution on the part of children "dummy numbers." Dummy numbers are numbers that children write when they are aware that an additional element should be included in their writing but are unsure of what digit to include. Alvarado and Ferreiro have identified several uses of dummy numbers: They have found a high frequency of the use of zero as a dummy number, a consistent use of one same dummy number in different written numbers, and a variation in the dummy number used in each of the numbers the children write. In George's case reported above, he said he was missing the teen, and then wrote zero and subsequently identified the zero as being the teen in the number. Quinteros (1997) has also reported on the use of dummy letters by young children. According to Quinteros, when children use dummy letters,

> they are unsure of having used the adequate letter, but use them anyway and
> these letters come to function as dummy letters. These dummies . . . are in-

cluded to substitute for a letter they are sure should be included in the written word, without knowing which it is. (p. 39)

This is paralleled in the case of George, who was aware that something was missing in his written number, but wasn't sure which digit to include and subsequently decided to include zero. George knew that if he only wrote a 9 for 19, an 8 for 18, or a 7 for 17, something would be missing from his writing. These digits on their own could not represent teen numbers such as 19, 18, or 17. He chose to represent the teen part of the number with the symbol 0. To us, this symbol is a zero, but we cannot be sure, from the interview data, what this symbol represented for George, beyond standing in for teen. George's example also shows that he knew that *different* numbers (such as 9 and 19) needed to be represented in *different* ways. George knew that 9 was a digit of 19, and knew that some part of the number, the part that sounds like "teen," was missing. By writing a zero he found a way to represent the missing part without necessarily being aware of what he was representing (a ten) or the meaning of the digit he was using.

We can only speculate about *why* George used zero to represent the teen. One speculation could be that the zero was taken from the ten that the teen was standing for—instead of taking the one from ten to represent the teen, he took the zero from ten. From the data available from George's interview, there is no way of knowing whether this was George's intention or not. It is also important to consider, as was mentioned, the data available from Alvarado and Ferreiro (2000) regarding Mexican children's frequent use of zero as a dummy number, because, as they mention, zero has a special status: "It is a special number, an almost-number because it is not used for counting" (p. 12).

Regarding the point made earlier about his knowledge of written numbers versus the kinds of written marks that he makes, we can see that George did understand important things about the way the system works, things that he was probably not taught directly or explicitly:

- There are both one- and two-digit numbers.
- Numbers with different names need to be written differently.
- The digits he knew (1 through 9) form part of two-digit numbers.
- Zero either as a number or as a graphic mark (from the interview data we are unsure of what status the zero had for George) could form part of a two-digit number.

In the larger sample from which George's example was taken, in two different tasks that required children to produce two-digit numbers, a third of the children used dummy numbers to stand for the parts of the numbers that they were unsure how to represent.

Furthermore, in the study of 30 kindergarten children from which George's interview was selected (Brizuela, 2001), most of the children wrote two-digit numbers with two digits. Remarkably, in all of the 30 interviews that were carried out, there were only three instances in which children did not write two-digit numbers with two digits. Marcos wrote 41 as 401; Cory wrote 52 as 1321; and Mikey wrote 41 as 144. The writing of 41 as 401—or of 301 as 3001 and of 1,002 as 10002—has been reported elsewhere as an inclusion of the "tens" or "hundreds," and so on, in the writing of the number (Lerner & Sadovsky, 1994; Scheuer, Sinclair, Merlo de Rivas, & Tièche Christinat, 2000). When I asked the children to write two-digit numbers, the only information they were given for how to write the number was the name of the number. Even numbers such as 60, which could be considered to be less transparent (the child would have to identify what elements there are in 60—a 6 [for six 10s] and a zero [for zero units]) were written with two digits. The *transparency* of a number has to do with the possibility that a naive speaker has of identifying the elements that make up a composite written number from its name. Haas (1996) explains that numbers are written in a temporal order that is decreasing—from the larger elements to the smaller ones. Most numbers also follow this decreasing temporal order in their enunciation, and there are practical reasons for this: With larger numbers, when we follow a decreasing temporal order in naming the number, we are naming first the element that represents the largest value. Greenberg (1978) explains that in languages that use Hindu-Arabic numbers, smaller numbers are usually verbally named in the smaller + larger order (in 14, the smaller digit, 4, is named before the larger one, even though we write the larger digit before the smaller one). Each language has a cut-off, which in English is 20: Before 20, composite numbers are spoken in the smaller + larger order, and after 20, in the larger + smaller order. Greenberg (1978) explains that "there is evidently a cognitive principle involved in the favoring of the order larger + smaller. . . . The opposite order leaves the hearer in the dark till the last item is reached" (p. 274).

Here, transparent numbers will be those that follow in writing and in speaking the larger + smaller temporal order, as well as those in which the elements of the written numbers can be identified from the spoken numbers.

Along similar lines, in another study, carried out by Mónica Alvarado (2002), 25 kindergarten students were interviewed and asked to produce two-digit numbers in isolation, without any reference to a specific quantity: telephone numbers, for example, "thirty-six, eleven, twenty-five." In this task, of the 350 productions of numbers that were dictated, 345 were written with two digits, even if the productions were not conventional. The five productions that did not use two digits followed an additive writing of numbers, for example, writing 108 for 18.

THE ROLE OF RELATIVE POSITION IN GEORGE'S IDEAS ABOUT WRITTEN NUMBERS

Place value constitutes an essential aspect of our written number system. It is a feature that has been considered one of the most important inventions and contributions to the number system. The complexity for children of the place value aspect of our number system has been recognized by both elementary school teachers and educational researchers (C. Kamii, 1985, 1989, 2000; M. Kamii, 1980; Lerner, 1994; Ross, 1986). Researchers have stated, for example, that

> while children are introduced to the meaning of "tens and ones" as early as first grade . . . numerous studies have documented that children's understanding of place value is generally poor throughout the primary grades. (Ross, 1986, p. 1)

> Place value is too difficult for first graders, and extremely confusing for second and even third graders to understand. Grouping objects and dealing with large quantities is one problem, but coordinating grouped quantities with the numeration system is quite another. (Kamii, 1980, p. 12)

> Place value is finally mastered by only half of the children in fourth grade. (Kamii, 1989, p. 14)

> The initial introduction of the decimal system and the positional notation system based on it is, by common agreement of educators, the most difficult instructional task in mathematics in the early school years. (Resnick, 1983, p. 126)

Furthermore, the understanding of the numerical place value system is important for other areas of mathematical learning, such as computations, exponentiations (Confrey, 1991, 1994; Lampert, 1989), and decimal fractions (Aaboe, 1964). At the same time, "constructing an understanding of place value necessarily implies comprehending other aspects of our written number system" (Sinclair & Scheuer, 1993, p. 200). Because of the place value feature of our number system, there is a geometric progression of the base as you move from place to place in a number (that is, for every place that a digit is moved to the left, its value is multiplied by a constant factor of 10), and there is a relationship between the value of a digit and the value of the place it is in (Confrey, 1991; Lampert, 1989). These features are translated into a certain notation: a finite number of symbols or digits (from zero to 9) are used, and these digits are combined in different ways to express all integers; the value of the number is determined by the position that each of the digits occupies.

As I stated above, research in mathematics education has identified that students do not really grasp place value until they are in lower elementary school (C. Kamii, 1985, 1989, 2000; M. Kamii, 1980; Lerner, 1994; Ross, 1986). However, I believe that the genesis of place value has previously not been thoroughly explored. While young children may not fully understand place value as a rule governing our number system, they may be able to begin to develop ideas about the importance of place and position in written numbers. In their own names, for example, very young children know that the first and last letters are different. The first letter in a name is a very important letter, thus acquiring a special status. As I've mentioned before, children build a logic about the written number system that parallels the logic of the system itself. If they do not ignore other aspects of the system's logic, why would they ignore this specific aspect, that of place value?

In his interview, George started out by not focusing on the position of the digits in the numbers he wrote. For example, he wrote 01 for 10 (see Figure 2.3), and I asked him the following questions:

BÁRBARA: Which is this one? (Pointing to 01 in his writing for 10.)
GEORGE: Ten (pointing to 01).
BÁRBARA: Ten? And this one? (Pointing to 10, printed on a card I presented him with)
GEORGE: Ten.
BÁRBARA: They're both ten?
GEORGE: Yeah.
BÁRBARA: But look, this one starts with a one (pointing to 10 printed on the card I had given him); this one starts with a zero (pointing to 01 in his writing for 10).
GEORGE: The zero . . .
BÁRBARA: Which is ten?
GEORGE: (Points to 01, his 10)
BÁRBARA: And this one? (Pointing to 10 on the card I had given him.)
GEORGE: One zero.
BÁRBARA: It's not ten. (George agrees) So it doesn't make a difference if it starts with a zero, right? (Pointing to 01)
GEORGE: Yeah.

For George, the position of the different digits in a number was a volatile factor in distinguishing between numbers. At first, he did not distinguish between 01 and 10, indicating that he did not differentiate between these two numbers based on digit position. Later, however, probably at my suggestion, George decided that 10 and 01 were different numbers, indicating that the order of placement of the digits in the number was beginning to make a difference for him. For the first time in the interview, he acknowledged that if the digits were in a different position, then the number would be different. Before this moment, however, he had not had to compare numbers. When he had to compare numbers, position became relevant. What also became evident in my questions, such as the one about 01 "starting" with zero, was that "starting" did not mean the same thing for George, because position of the digits was not constant or prominent for him. In the following excerpt, I wrote three numbers for George (Figure 2.7); the three numbers were different, but they each contained the same elements or digits, in different positions. I wrote each of these numbers and asked George to compare them:

> BÁRBARA: OK. So how about this number, George? Look at this one. Do you think one of these is more? (Writing 273 and 237 [Figure 2.7])
> GEORGE: I think this one's more (pointing to 273).
> BÁRBARA: Why? The one on the top?

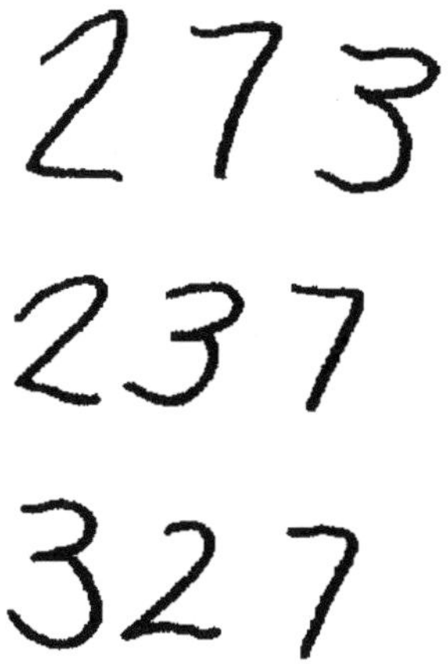

$$273$$

$$237$$

$$327$$

Figure 2.7. My writing of numbers for George to compare.

GEORGE: Yeah.

BÁRBARA: Why?

GEORGE: 'Cause this one (pointing to the 7 in 273) [is] more than these two (pointing to the 2 and the 3 in 237). 'Cause these were the highest numbers (pointing to the 7 in each 237 and 273).

BÁRBARA: This one is the highest number? The seven? Or the . . . (pointing to the 7 in 273).

GEORGE: These two are the highest (pointing to the 7 in 273 and in 237). This one's higher (pointing to 7 in 273), then that's the biggest (pointing to 273).

BÁRBARA: How do you know?

GEORGE: Because, I just don't know how I know that.

When he had to compare two numbers that had the same amount of elements in them and the same digits, he decided to focus on the individual digits in the number. Since 273 had a 7 in it, he decided that 273 was more. He disregarded the fact that this argument did not hold if 237 *also* had a 7 in it. In deciding that 273 was more, George was beginning to focus on the *position* of the digits as a criterion for deciding which number was more, since 273 was the only number where the 7 was in the middle position. Following the events in this excerpt, I asked George to compare other three-digit numbers:

BÁRBARA: And this one? (Pointing to 573 that I had presented to him on a card)

GEORGE: A high number.

BÁRBARA: A high number? But which one is more? This one or this one? (Pointing to 573 and 134, on two different cards)

GEORGE: (Points to 134 on a card)

BÁRBARA: Why? How do you know?

. . .

GEORGE: 'Cause that's a four (pointing to the 4 in 134), and that one has a three (pointing to the 3 in 573).

. . .

BÁRBARA: So this one is more, you think? (Pointing to 134)

GEORGE: (Nods head yes)

By comparing the *last* digit in 134 and 573, George decided that 134 was more because 4 was more than 3. He maintained this position in spite of the fact that I pushed him to look at and compare other digits in the number. This analysis of single digits was similar to the analysis that he had originally made of 273 and 237, in which he was comparing the single digits in the two numbers to decide which was more. In the case of his comparison of 573 and 134, he was clearly focused on comparing the single digits. Furthermore, in this case he focused on comparing digits in the *same position*. So, position began to be important when comparing numbers, as it was with 10 and 01. The comparison of 573 and 134, however, was more complex than that of 10 and 01 or of 273 and 237, because this first pair of numbers did not have the same digits or elements in them.

The written number system is formed by a finite set of elements, which can, in turn, be combined to form infinite numbers. The following excerpt shows how George was aware of the limits posed by the system itself on his production of numbers.

BÁRBARA: Do you think *you* could invent a new number?
GEORGE: Yeah.
BÁRBARA: Yeah? Like which one?
GEORGE: Like a new seven.
BÁRBARA: A new seven? A new way to draw a seven?
GEORGE: A new eight. A new nine, a new ten, and a new eleven.
BÁRBARA: Do you want to show me a new seven?
GEORGE: Yeah.
BÁRBARA: Show me a new seven.
GEORGE: (Writes 7, tilted to the side [Figure 2.8a])
BÁRBARA: What makes it new?
GEORGE: 'Cause it's pointing that way (conventionally), and that one's (the one he had written earlier [see Figure 2.2g]) pointing that way (it's in mirror image).
BÁRBARA: Oh, I see. That makes it new. Could you make a new eight?

(a) 7   (b) 8

Figure 2.8. George's new numbers.

GEORGE: (Writes 8, trying to make it as a curving line instead of the two circles that he had previously made [see Figures 2.2h and 2.8b])

BÁRBARA: What makes it new?

GEORGE: (Pause)

BÁRBARA: But how can people know which one is which?

GEORGE: I don't know.

Here, George found a *figurative* differentiation of the numbers 7 and 8. What determined that they were new numbers for him was that they *looked* different and that they had a different shape. However, because figurative and operative aspects cannot be isolated from each other in thought (see Fraisse & Piaget, 1969; Piaget, 1961/1969; Piaget & Inhelder, 1966/1971, 1968/1973), we can also assume that there was knowledge about the written number system that backed up this figurative transformation of the numbers: He knew about the elements of the written number system and therefore found that only figurative transformations of them could result in "new" numbers. In order to create a "new" number, George worked on the set of numbers he already knew.

REFLECTIONS

This interview with George shows how in spite of his young age and the many difficulties he had in writing numbers, he had developed important ideas about how the written number system works, specifically regarding the role of position in numbers, and the elements that form the system. As teachers of children like George, we might be prone to underestimate how much they already know and how much more they are capable of learning about written numbers. His young age and his imperfect fine-motor skills were not good indicators of the complexity of his thinking and understanding. As will be shown in the following two chapters, in the examples of Paula and Thomas, young children construct very complex understandings about written numbers and the written number system.

Paula: "Capital Numbers"

PAULA: Capital letters and capital numbers.
BÁRBARA: What are capital numbers?
PAULA: Thirty-three. So thirty is a capital number of three. And that's the other way to write the three (pointing to the 3 in the tens place).

In mathematics education, conventional knowledge and children's invented, idiosyncratic ideas are oftentimes considered to be unrelated and unconnected aspects of knowledge; the first are learned by transmission, while the second are *created* by subjects. This position presents a dichotomy of conventions and inventions. This dichotomy affects the perceptions that we as educators develop regarding conventions such as mathematical notations.

Much literature in mathematics education does not consider the process involved in learning mathematical notations to be a *constructive* process. The learning of notations is thought to be automatic, a result of understandings developed about mathematical concepts. Learning notations is thought to be a *consequence* of learning concepts. In this chapter, Paula highlights, through her "capital numbers," the constructive aspects of learning mathematical notations; her case also illustrates the cooperation, collaboration, and interaction that takes place between conventional knowledge, such as notations, and inventions, such as children's invented mathematical notations, indicating that both aspects of knowledge are necessarily complementary. My argument in this chapter will be twofold: first, children's invented notations are of utmost importance in children's learning and development of notations; second, conventional notations play an important role in children's invented notations and provide a support for their development. At the same time, they are subordinate to inventions and to the assimilatory aspects of thought. This position borrows from Piaget's perspective regarding the figurative and operative aspects of thought, which he considered to be complementary (1972; Gruber & Vonèche, 1977; Piaget & Inhelder, 1966/1971, 1968/1973), as well as Ferreiro's (1986a) work and her perspective regarding the assimilation of conventional information in the area of written language. Piaget (1972) defines figurative aspects of thought as "an imitation of states taken as momentary and static," while the operative aspect "deals not with states but with transformations from one state to another" (p. 14).

In the analysis of the protocols from extended clinical interviews (Duckworth, 1996) that were carried out with Paula, I will focus on her making sense of the conventional written number system and on the roles that the conventions and her own invented ideas played in that sense-making.

MAKING SENSE OF CONVENTIONS

Paula, who requested that her real name be used, was a 5-year-old child who attended a public kindergarten. She was the only child of a middle-class family. A bright child, she related easily to both children and adults. She was extremely lively and tended to adopt leading roles in different environments—with neighbors, at kindergarten, and at her after-school program.

A series of four interviews were carried out with Paula. During 3 months, interviews were held every 3 weeks, and each lasted between 30 and 45 minutes. Each interview was videotaped and later transcribed verbatim. In each interview, Paula was presented with different kinds of materials (coins, pencil and paper, dice, tags with numbers printed on them) and with questions related to the number system and its notational aspects. Although the questions that were presented to Paula were not fully determined before the beginning of the interview, I did have in mind a series of areas to explore.

During our first interview, Paula wrote numbers from 1 to 12 and counted from 1 to 28. At first, when I asked her to write numbers beyond 12, she would say that she did not know how to do that, and there seemed to be no pattern in the way that she named numbers beyond 12. She could give a number a certain name (usually not conventional), and then name it as something different a few minutes later.

During our first interview, Paula provided various examples of her knowledge of certain mathematical conventions and of how social information had possibly contributed to her construction and understanding of these conventions. For example, she told me that she could write numbers from 1 to 12 and that she knew them because the clock in her house had those numbers.

During our second interview, I showed Paula nine paper tags with a number from 1 to 9 printed on each one, and then I posed a question.

BÁRBARA: Of all these numbers, Paula, which one is more?
PAULA: The nine.
BÁRBARA: Why?
PAULA: *Because it goes* one, two, three, four, five, six, seven, eight, *nine*. So this one (pointing to tag 9) is more. (Emphasis added)

Later, I gave Paula three more tags, with numbers 10, 11, and 12 printed on them. Paula took the tags and spontaneously placed them, in a row, in a series in ascending order, from 1 to 12. I asked her what she had done.

PAULA: I made the numbers *like in the real world.*
BÁRBARA: Like where?
PAULA: *Like real counting.* (Emphasis added)

In these excerpts, we can gather that Paula has developed the idea that there is an order to numbers, one that must be followed, and that is already determined, "in the real world." Paula has had access to conventional knowledge, and she has developed her own personal ideas about this information she has interacted with. During this same interview, I wrote the numbers 48 and 100 (Figure 3.1) and put a question to Paula.

BÁRBARA: Can you think of what numbers they (pointing to 100 and 48) could be?
PAULA: No.
BÁRBARA: Try to imagine, which number is this one (pointing to 100)?
PAULA: One hundred.
BÁRBARA: This one *is* one hundred. How do you know?
PAULA: *Because I have a book that has that, and it says "one hundred."* (Emphasis added)

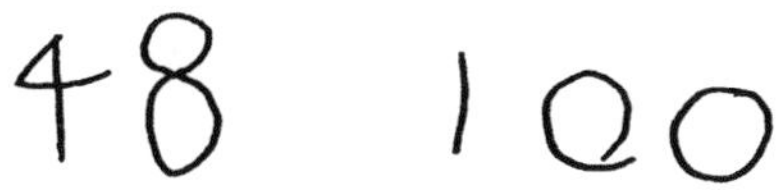

48   100

Figure 3.1. "Forty-eight and one hundred—how do you read these numbers?"

In this example, Paula showed what other sources of information from the "real world"—such as books—she has used to develop an understanding of the number system. During our following interview, I asked her to write 34.

> BÁRBARA: Try to think of it before you write it. What would it look like?
>
> PAULA: I know.
>
> BÁRBARA: You know? Did you already think of it, in your mind (using Paula's own phrase [see Piaget, 1976])?
>
> PAULA: Yeah (picking up the pencil and starting to write). Yep. You know what (she stops writing), I know, I didn't even think in my mind, but every time I watch TV in my house, thir . . . , I have to put kid's channel, I have to put three four. And then if it . . . every time they say I have to do thirty-four I do like . . . (and she writes 34 [Figure 3.2]).

Paula took information from different sources with which she was in contact every day: a clock, books, TV. In interaction with the information provided by these sources, she "taught herself" (as she argued) how to write numbers from 1 to 12, and she constructed the idea that there is a certain order to numbers, a way that "numbers go in the real world." In addition, she developed the idea that in that order, the last numbers are "more": When I asked her which was more in a series of numbers from 1 to 9, she named the whole set and finished off with 9, and she claimed that therefore 9 had to be more, since it was at the end of the series. Further, her naming of the number 34 as thirty-four also shows that she was aware of conventions: She first said it was a 3 and a 4, but she was not satisfied with giving it that name and named it, conventionally, as "thirty-four."

These examples illustrate how Paula coordinated information, that she assimilated from her environment, with her previous knowledge, in the

Figure 3.2. Paula's 34—her mother's age and the kids' channel.

process of solving certain dilemmas—how to write 34, what the number 100 is. Faced with these dilemmas, Paula used information from the environment (the tags with which she was faced, for example), coordinated it with previous knowledge, such as the number for the kid's channel, and constructed something new: how to write 34. The numbers on the clock and the numbers 100 and 34 were not simply being socially transmitted or "copied." Each "piece of information" was integrated with the rest and was transformed. At the same time, the pieces of information became integrated into her existing mental structure, together with her previous knowledge: Paula used the information when appropriate; it had not been copied but rather assimilated and reconstructed. Furthermore, she was able to use the information she had assimilated in a particular context, faced with a particular need, thus illustrating the way in which the information was truly assimilated by her.

CAPITAL NUMBERS: PAULA'S INVENTED TOOL

In the events that followed, Paula was asked to deal mainly with two-digit numbers (beyond the 10, 11, and 12 that she could write conventionally). Faced with this new dilemma, Paula's inventions played an important role. During our second interview, Paula wrote 310 (Figure 3.3a) and told me that it said "twenty-one." Then, during our third meeting, I asked Paula to write "two hundred," and she wrote 08 (see Figure 3.3b). She then wrote 38 (see Figure 3.3c) and said, "I don't know" when I asked her what number that was. A few minutes later, when I wrote 48 (Figure 3.4a) and asked her what number it was, the following dialogue took place:

PAULA: Thirty-one, thirt . . . (pause)
BÁRBARA: Which one could it be?
PAULA: Forty-eight.
BÁRBARA: You're right Paula, that number is forty-eight. How did you know?
PAULA: Because, I like . . . I was doing like this (putting her hands at the sides of her head), I was thinking in my mind, and I was doing like this . . . (pause) what if, what if you write another number here, do another number there (pointing to the paper).
BÁRBARA: OK. (I write 46 [Figure 3.4b])
PAULA: I was thinking like this (puts her hands at the sides of her head and looks at the number). Forty-six (speaking slowly).
BÁRBARA: But how do you think like that?

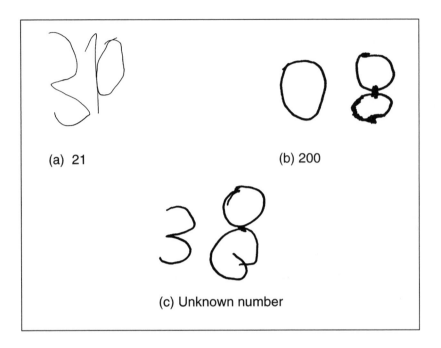

Figure 3.3. Paula's writing of two- and three-digit numbers.

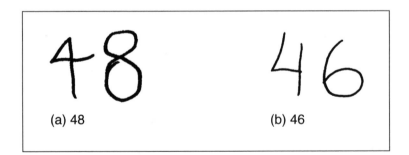

Figure 3.4. Paula's identification of two-digit numbers.

PAULA: Because I just know in my mind.
BÁRBARA: Can you teach me how to do that, so I know how to do that also?
PAULA: Yeah, just . . .
BÁRBARA: How do you know what sound it is, like, what to say?
PAULA: Because I just know that it's, first I say a four and then I say a six, and then I say: Ah! Forty-six!!

During the course of our interview, Paula began to develop a system for interpreting two-digit numbers. She was successful in reading the numbers conventionally, but still was not able to explain how she was able to do it. Once again, we see her process of naming: In this excerpt we see that she was not comfortable with calling 46 "four, six," just as she was not comfortable earlier with calling 34 "three, four"—at this young age she was already aware of the *accepted* conventional names for numbers. She also first attempted to say "thirty-one, thirt . . . " for 48. She knew it could not be named as "four, eight." It is possible that Paula was thinking that the name for the number needed to be something like "thirty, forty" something with " . . . ty," possibly associating these names with two-digit numbers.

After this, Paula wrote 34. As you may recall, 34 was a number Paula knew both how to name and how to write, mainly because it was her mother's age as well as the kid's channel she watched on TV. I then asked her a question.

BÁRBARA: How do you read that? How do say that number?
PAULA: You say . . . first you think of a three, and then you do like a capital letter but instead of a capital, a capital number, so it's thirty-four (pronouncing slowly).
BÁRBARA: So this one (I point to 31, which I had written previously [Figure 3.5]), what number could this one be?
PAULA: Thirty-three . . . Thirty-one!
BÁRBARA: Thirty-one. Yeah. (Pause) Is that right? Is that thirty-one?

Figure 3.5. Paula's identification of 31.

(Wanting to confuse her and wanting to make sure *she* was sure that the number was thirty-one.)

PAULA: Hey, now I know, because you made two threes in each one (pointing to 34 and 31) and that's a three (pointing to the 3 in the tens place in 31), I remember how to do a three now, and now I know how to do thirty-three!

BÁRBARA: (Wanting to confuse her) Do you know how to write thirty-three? Which one was this one (pointing to 31)? I got confused.

PAULA: Thirty-three . . . what is the capital of three, in this number (pointing to 31)?

BÁRBARA: You said . . . how much was this one (pointing to 31)?

PAULA: What was the capital of one again?

BÁRBARA: Why do you call them capitals?

PAULA: Thirty!! . . . One.

BÁRBARA: Why do you call them capitals?

PAULA: Capital *letters* and capital *numbers*.

BÁRBARA: What are capital numbers?

PAULA: Like, if I write a little, little number (Figure 3.6), it could be a capital one, it could be a little number . . . it's not really like that . . . It's really like . . . capital is another way . . . this is one way how to write an *E*, right? (see Figure 3.7, left.)

BÁRBARA: Yeah.

PAULA: And then this is another way how to write an *e* (see Figure 3.7, right). That's capital.

BÁRBARA: Which one is capital (confused because Paula has reversed what should be a capital letter and what should be a lowercase letter)?

PAULA: This one (pointing to the lowercase letter).

BÁRBARA: So which one of these is capital (pointing to the 31 [see Figure 3.6])? Of the numbers?

PAULA: I say this one (points to the lowercase *e* again). . . . Of the numbers?

BÁRBARA: Yeah.

PAULA: Thirty-three. So *thirty* is a *capital* number of three. And that's the other way to write the three (pointing to the 3 in the tens place in 31 [see Figure 3.6]).

$$31$$

Figure 3.6. "A little, little number."

Figure 3.7. Two ways to write an *e*.

Paula's capital numbers came to function as a tool for her. In this instance, the tool she constructed helped her move beyond her prior understandings and performances, thus highlighting the Vygotskian notion of the profound impact of tools on cognitive processes and products (Vygotsky, 1978, 1986). Recently, Meira (2002) has explored ways in which tools such as notations help to augment children's cognitive processes. This seems to have been the case with Paula's capital numbers.

INVENTIONS

Learning and constructing knowledge involve inventions—novel productions we create, using our present cognitive structures, while trying to make sense of a situation or phenomena. Certain features of the situation are assimilated; and as a result of the interaction between what previously existed and what is assimilated—through the reciprocal assimilation (Piaget, 1936/1952) of the existing and the novel schemas—the learner *invents*. But the knowledge that results from these interactions is "richer than what the objects can provide by themselves" (Piaget, 1970, p. 713).

In this sense, Ferreiro has highlighted the "interplay between assimilation and information":

> Social practices as well as social information are not received passively by children. When they try to understand, they necessarily transform the content received. Moreover, in order to register the information, they transform it. This is the deep meaning of the notion of *assimilation* that Piaget has put at the core of his theory. (Ferreiro, 1986a, p. 16; emphasis in original)

That is, children need to invent in order to understand and to assimilate information. Of course the information provided by the environment is important and plays a pivotal role, but it is not the end-all of the learning process.

The idea of capital numbers was invented on the basis of the information and knowledge that Paula had previously developed about numbers, as well as the knowledge she had about capital letters: Paula knew that capital letters were a graphic differentiation of lowercase letters, and thus a capital letter was the same as a lowercase letter in one sense, but different as well. We can also assume, because she could write her name conventionally, that she knew that certain kinds of letters (which to us are uppercase, or capital, letters) precede and are placed at the left of the writing of some words (such as her name). The disequilibrium of not being able to provide a conventional reading for two-digit numbers beyond 12 incited Paula to go "in search of new solutions" (Inhelder, Sinclair, & Bovet, 1974, p. 264), namely, the idea of capital numbers.

Inventions must be analyzed in the context of the situation that is being assimilated, and of the dilemma that is being faced, in order to be understood by those who are not their creators. At the same time, children's inventions should be fostered and respected (Bamberger, 1991; Confrey, 1991; Ferreiro, 1986b; Sinclair, 1982).

Piaget (1970) has regarded inventions as central to knowledge construction, and as characterizing "all living thought" (p. 714). He has stated, for example:

> *The problem we must solve, in order to explain cognitive development, is that of invention and not of mere copying.* And neither stimulus-response generalization nor the introduction of transformational responses can explain novelty or invention. By contrast, the concepts of assimilation and accommodation and of operational structures (which are *created*, not merely discovered, as a result of the subject's activities), are oriented toward *this inventive construction which characterizes all living thought.* (pp. 713–714; emphasis added)
>
> Genuine optimism would consist of believing in the child's capacities for invention. Remember also that each time that one prematurely teaches a child something he could have discovered for himself, that child is kept from inventing it and consequently from understanding it completely. (p. 715)

The history of mathematics provides us with examples of the role that innovation and creation have played in the development of the discipline. For example, although the Babylonians of circa 2100 B.C. used a blank space to indicate zero, and eventually a special symbol during the Seleucid period (300–1 B.C.), it was not until about A.D. 900 that a sign for zero that is comparable to the symbol we use for zero today was developed, by the Hindus. Whereas the Babylonian symbol only occurred between digits, the Hindu zero also appeared at the end of a number (Struik, 1987). Through this example I wish to illustrate that mathematics, as it exists today, owes much to creative and inventive individuals throughout history. In addition, individuals' inventions form part of a coherent whole in the context of their mental structures; and these inventions can be understood as individuals' attempts to make sense of situations.

We are constantly in contact with different kinds of conventions: conventions in reading, writing, mathematics, music, science. At some point in history, a convention was someone's invention—"a unique achievement . . . a form of organization within a domain that has never before been accomplished in quite the same way" (Feldman, 1994, p. 11). This invention developed into a convention once its use became widespread because of its utility, because it facilitated tasks in some way. Mathematical conventions, for example, make it easier to keep track of things, to carry out computations, and to deal with large numbers (Kilpatrick, 1985). To the learner who is faced with having to use certain conventions, without being given a chance to make sense of them, conventions seem totally arbitrary. Historically, however, there *is* a reason for their adoption. Reflecting on the continuity between invented and conventional notations can possibly lead us to begin to give children opportunities to make sense of conventions, to appropriate them, and to make them their own.

CONVENTIONS

The system of numbers and written numbers that Paula interacted with had an impact on the kinds of ideas that she developed and the kinds of inventions she created. I am not at all advocating a transmission kind of explanation. But the system that Paula interacted with has certain rules, and Paula will gradually appropriate these rules, building personal understandings and making the rules her own. For instance, *position* is a feature of the written number system. There are a finite number of elements that constitute the system, and these elements can be found, at times, occupying different positions. Therefore, Paula's ideas about numbers and their capitals, and the attention that she was paying to relative position and its importance in the written number system, make perfect sense. Similarly, in Chapter 2 we saw how George began to pay attention to the relative position of elements of numbers. A second feature of the written number system that Paula paid attention to and generated ideas about was the finite number of elements in the system: 10 elements. In her invention of the idea of capital numbers, Paula may have brought together an implicit understanding about this rule regarding the written number system. Given that the elements in the system cannot be changed, in capital numbers different combinations of the elements are named differently. Alvarado (2002) made a similar observation when she found children who would intentionally rotate digits in the tens place of two-digit numbers, even though they would not use the same rotation if they wrote the same digit in the ones place or as a single isolated digit. The children explained that the rotation served to differentiate between a 3 and a 30 or a 4 and a 40, for example. These children are also interacting with these same rules of the written number system and creating their own inventions to make sense of these conventional rules. They, in fact, are creating their own, parallel rules.

REFLECTIONS

During our conversations, Paula was faced with trying to read and write numbers beyond 12. She had a clock to help her with numbers from 1 to 12, but she had no "ready-made" tool to help her beyond that. She thus constructed a tool (Vygotsky, 1978, 1986), her capital numbers, that allowed her to offer a reading of numbers that was conventional (she read 48 and 46 conventionally). This tool was useful to her because it helped her to read and write two-digit numbers, to make sense of conventional numerical notations, and to find a pattern in the way that numbers are written. How did she construct this tool?

In a sense, Paula was asked to go beyond the realm in which she felt comfortable. She was not satisfied with calling 31 "three one"; she knew that this name was not correct. While trying to provide a conventional or at least satisfying (to her) interpretation, she developed the idea of capital numbers. Her capital numbers brought together many ideas. First, Paula showed, through her capital numbers, that she distinguished between the positions occupied by different numbers: It was not the same for a number to be in the far right or units place (even if she didn't call them this) than to be in the far left or tens place (she only made this distinction between units and tens, and did not go into decimals, or hundreds, thousands, and so on). The position occupied by numbers makes them different in some way. We could argue that her thinking went along the following lines: If numbers are in different positions or are in some way different, then they should also have different names.

Further, in her capital numbers, Paula exemplifies the types of relationships children establish between numbers and letters. In capital numbers, Paula coordinated knowledge from apparently distinct realms: language and mathematics. Historians such as Neugebauer (1945) and Struik (1987) have also made connections between these realms. They compare the alphabet and the place value system because both inventions came to replace a complex symbolism by a method easily understood by a large number of people. Positional notation is "one of the most fertile inventions of humanity," comparable to "the invention of the alphabet" (Neugebauer, 1962, p. 5). Similarly, Alvarado and Ferreiro (2000) have highlighted that "we must understand the intricate relations that, in the course of evolution, numbers and letters maintain between them: two *different* but also *related* systems" (p. 17; emphasis added).

At 5 years of age, Paula could already distinguish between numbers and letters. She showed this when I asked her to write numbers and she wrote numbers; when we spoke of letters (capital and lowercase letters), she wrote only letters. In spite of this differentiation she established, when she developed the idea of capital numbers, she "borrowed" from the area of written language. This borrowing embodies, in a way, our adult view of things. For her it may simply have been a way of obtaining access to her current knowledge repertoire. In this interview excerpt, Paula made explicit a hypothesis that she had developed about the written number system and how it worked: that each number had a "capital" that corresponds to it. The position that the numbers were written in determined whether or not numbers were "capital" and therein what number it was and how it would be read. This hypothesis allowed Paula to begin to read and write two-digit numbers systematically.

Underlying Paula's statements was the hypothesis that units were different from tens, or at least that the position that a digit occupied changed what number it was (3 or 30, for example). In developing this hypothesis, Paula borrowed from written language the terminology of *capital letters*. Similar to the case of numbers and their capitals, each letter has a capital that corresponds to it; lowercase and capital letters are the same but also different; and it is also true that their position in a word can sometimes determine whether they are capital letters (even though the name Paula provided for lowercase and capital letters was reversed).

There was also a difference between capital letters and capital numbers that Paula may not have been aware of: Capital letters have the same meaning as their corresponding lowercase letter (e.g., *E* and *e*; *A* and *a*), but have a different written form. Capital numbers, on the other hand, have the same written form as their corresponding unit number (e.g., the 1 in 10 and in 1, the 2 in 20 and in 2), but have a different meaning. In trying to solve a dilemma she faced, Paula borrowed from wherever she could, without restricting herself necessarily to the area of numbers exclusively. From language she borrowed the existence of capital letters and some of their characteristics (that they occupy different positions in words, that they are important in reading, and that they are "another way" of writing letters). She then coordinated this knowledge with knowledge from mathematics: that the same digits have different names according to the position they occupy, that there is a certain order to numbers, that "in the real world" there is a "given" way to read numbers. She transformed the knowledge as it existed before and coordinated it with the dilemma that she was faced with (*how can I read those notations?*), in order to solve it.

As a result of the activities of comparing, transforming, and coordinating, and of the interaction between her invention and the conventions, Paula made up her own hypothesis regarding capital numbers. In her hypothesis, there was a pattern to numerical notation: Each digit had a capital number that corresponded to it, and the relationship between the names of digits and their capitals was transparent. Again, as Alvarado (2002) has shown in her research, establishing connections between language and mathematics is relevant methodologically and cognitively, as it has been historically as well.

This same pattern and construction will, probably, lead Paula to further learning and knowledge construction. For example, she stated that she "did not know" which were the capitals of 1, 2, and 5. In these numbers, the relationship between the names of digits and their capitals is not as transparent (or is opaque, as Alvarado [2002] would say) to Paula: The relationship of 1 to 13 and 14, for example, is not as transparent as that of 4 to 40 or 6 to 60. Neither are the relationships between 2 and 20, and 5 and 50. This is the case for English. In Japanese and Chinese, number words are more regular and systematic (e.g., in English we say "twelve, thirteen," whereas the Japanese say "ten-two, ten-three." See Kilpatrick, 1985). In the case of 3, Paula again used previous knowledge (both her mother's age and the kid's channel were 34), to construct the capital for this number (30, where the relationship to 3 is once again not transparent). Once she found it problematic that her invented tool, as it existed, could not help her to find the capital numbers for all digits, this would probably lead to cognitive conflict and to further development of her invented hypothesis about capital numbers and understanding of the written number system and how it works.

In summary, while conventions are important in learning, learners coordinate and assimilate (Piaget, 1970) them into an existing mental structure. They are integrated with the existing schemata and transformed (in addition, the assimilating mental structure is also transformed) or *reconstructed*. Inventions, assimilatory processes, and existing mental structures are pivots in the integration of those conventions into a coherent whole. In the field of music, Bamberger (1991; Bamberger & Ziporyn, 1992) adopts a similar perspective, and argues that "rules," or conventions, should not be thought of as static entities that have a "life and meaning of their own," because each person has a different interpretation of and use for them.

What is important is for learners to develop those multiple interpretations and representations of them, and become owners of those rules:

> Each individual displays . . . his or her own *version* of the rules, and this version will always differ from person to person. . . . The rules themselves are only interesting in that they allow for so many different ways to get them wrong. And since nobody is getting them right, the rules themselves are abstracted out of existence. (Bamberger & Ziporyn, 1992, p. 38; see also Piaget, 1966/1971, p. 380)

Both the conventions and the individual's creations play a part in the re-creation of socially accepted knowledge and in making sense of mathematical conventions. Knowledge about the conventional system, such as that of the notational aspects of mathematics, is constructed through the interaction between what the individual brings into the situation (the inventions) *and* what the greater social order presents to the learner (the conventions). But the emphasis must be placed on the *importance of children's inventions* in the processes of learning and knowledge construction, for it is through their constructions and assimilatory structures that individuals will be able to make sense of what is presented and that which is otherwise foreign—conventions. Through her inventions, Paula shows us that both inventions and conventions are fundamental in the construction of mathematical knowledge, and that although conventions depend on inventions, they also provide a support for their development. Through the interactions between conventions and inventions, inventions become richer and conventions are embedded with personal meaning for the learner. Thus, conventions can become tools for making sense of mathematics, instead of simply being arbitrary symbolizations. Conventions, then, can be reconstructed by children, through the interactions and coordinations between what they invent and what society provides to them. Inventing and creating are of utmost importance for knowledge construction. Why, then, should we reject children's inventions? Why not create the most appropriate situations in which they can develop?

Thomas: Commas and Periods in Numbers

THOMAS: If there are no periods . . . but they don't do anything! . . . The period just tells you to stop. . . . It's like a red light. It tells you to stop and read that.

Reading the preceding quote, we would not know for sure if we were referring to written language or numbers. In any case, we would most likely not think of numbers. Most often, periods and commas used in numbers are not considered to be a part of the written number system. However, these symbols are integral both to the way in which we represent numbers and to children's understanding of written numbers, as we will see in this chapter. In our everyday lives, numbers we see written have commas and periods integrated into them. These periods and commas refer both to the punctuation marks dividing whole and decimal parts of numbers and to the periods or commas marking the different place values in numbers (as in 2,000 or 1,000,000). Interestingly, the *kinds* of punctuation marks—periods, commas, colons, semicolons—used are arbitrary, and the use of commas or periods in numbers is not consistent across different parts of the world. For instance, in the United States periods are used to separate the decimal and whole parts of numbers, and commas are used to group digits in the whole parts of numbers. In other parts of the world, however, periods and commas are used in the opposite way. That is, commas are used to separate decimal and whole parts of numbers, and periods are used to group digits in the whole parts of numbers.

In this chapter I will focus on Thomas, who explored some written aspects of numbers that were related to the use of punctuation marks during the course of eight sessions that we spent together. When I began my interviews with Thomas, it was not my intention to work on these specific notational aspects of numbers. It was Thomas himself who determined this focus, because of the issues related to how written numbers work that he was struggling with at the time. I began the sessions interested in Thomas's thinking about written numbers and how the written number system works. I was not particularly interested in knowing *how much* the written numbers represented to him, or the *relation* between the numbers and a particular collection of objects. Instead, I was interested in understanding Thomas's thinking about how the written number system works.

I will organize my work with Thomas into two areas: the use of periods and commas to aid in the reading of numbers, and the use of periods and commas to organize the numbers graphically. These areas emerged from the analyses of the interviews and my questions about the kinds of struggles, questions, and constructive work involved in Thomas's learning about periods and commas.

At the time of the sessions, Thomas had recently turned 6, and he was finishing kindergarten and preparing to enter first grade. Thomas's parents told me, before I started meeting with him, that during the preceding year he had developed an interest in numbers and mathematics.

Each of the eight sessions was audiotaped, and a report was written about each one. In addition, I wrote weekly journals in which I reflected on the sessions Thomas and I had. The audiotapes, written productions that Thomas and I made during our meetings, session reports, and journals become the materials to develop this account.

For my work with Thomas, I used the extended clinical interviewing approach (Duckworth, 1996). I told Thomas that we would be talking about what he knew and thought about numbers. I took pencils, paper, crayons, blank cards, and cards with numbers printed on them to each one of our sessions together. During our interviews, my intent was not only to explore Thomas's thinking, but also to "engender conflicts" (Duckworth, 1996, p. 136) and to follow the development of Thomas's thinking as it was taking place. For example, during the interviews, when I identified contradictions in Thomas's thinking, I attempted to highlight these contradictions to further explore his thoughts about written numbers in general, and periods and commas in particular. The contents of the following sections are only excerpts of the interviews that took place, focusing on instances in which the use of periods and commas in numbers was discussed.

THOMAS'S DEVELOPING UNDERSTANDING OF PERIODS AND COMMAS IN NUMBERS

Although Thomas, at the time of the interviews, could already interpret and write many numbers in a conventional way, he was still in the process of developing hypotheses and systematic ideas about the written number system. That is, his learning of the written number system was not complete. Reading and writing numbers in a conventional way does not cover all there is to learn about numbers. For example, during the interviews, Thomas developed his own hypotheses about periods and commas. In

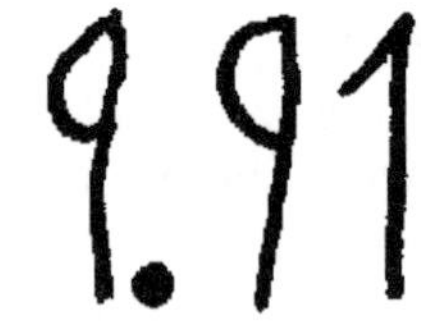

9.91

Figure 4.1. Thomas's writing of $9.91.

Thomas's case, these periods and commas were not confined to decimal fractions (as in 9.91), but also involved the signs we use in numbers beyond 999 (such as, for example, the comma in 1,000). In this chapter, however, I will not focus on the first aspect. It is worth mentioning, though, that from our very first session together, Thomas established a differentiation between these two aspects. In the first case, he confined his examples to the use of money and used the period to separate "dollars and cents." In this first session of work, Thomas wrote 9.91 (Figure 4.1) and read it as "nine dollars and ninety-one cents." When I asked Thomas about the period in the number he had written, he said that in 9.91 the period meant that the second part of the number was cents and the first part was dollars.

When we began our work together, Thomas was very comfortable writing and reading numbers in a conventional way. He managed to write numbers up to 10,000, and to read numbers conventionally up to the thousands (four-digit numbers). Our first session together was the first time that I saw Thomas write a number with a period in it. When I asked Thomas to write "a very difficult number," he wrote 1,000 as 1000 (Figure 4.2). Immediately afterward, Thomas wrote 10.000 (Figure 4.3) as an example of another "difficult number," and told me it said "ten thousand."

The Use of Periods and Commas to Aid in the Reading of Numbers

During our first sessions of work, Thomas consistently used *only* periods. In addition to the numbers mentioned above, he also wrote 100.1000 (Fig-

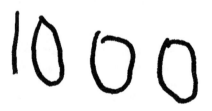

Figure 4.2. Thomas's writing of 1,000.

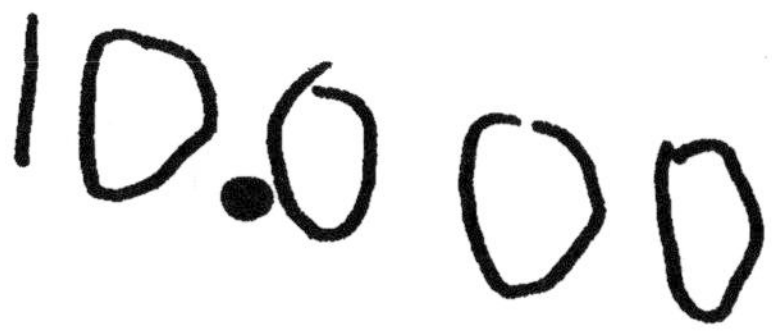

Figure 4.3. Thomas's writing of 10,000.

ure 4.4). He read these numbers as "ten thousand" (see Figure 4.3), "nine dollars and ninety-one cents" (see Figure 4.1), and "one hundred thousand" (see Figure 4.4), respectively. When I asked Thomas about the periods he was writing in the numbers, he said that in 10.000 the period let you know that 10,000 was 10,000 and not some other number. He also explained to me that if 100.1000 didn't have a period, then it would read as "one thousand and one" and not as "one hundred thousand." That is, without the period in it, Thomas would ignore the last three zeros in 100.1000 when reading the number. In the case of 9.91, he considered this to be a different kind of number, in other words, money.

From our first session of work together, Thomas began to develop his ideas about periods in numbers. The main way he thought about the periods in this first session was that they provided a way to *read* numbers; Thomas used periods to organize his *reading* of numbers. It was still unclear at this point, however, why he chose to *write* numbers with periods in them. We might hypothesize that in writing numbers with periods in them he was adjusting to the conventional information he had interacted with previously, regarding how numbers are written. This information, available to him, was, however, not enough to enable him to understand right away the conventional uses of punctuation marks in numbers.

In subsequent sessions of work, Thomas continued to elaborate on the idea that periods in numbers tell you what to read and what you should consider when reading a number. For example, when during our second session together I wrote 1.000.000 and 100.000.000.000, he read the first number as "one" and the second as "one hundred zero, zero, zero, zero, zero, zero, zero, zero." He also interpreted 1.000 as "one," and 1000

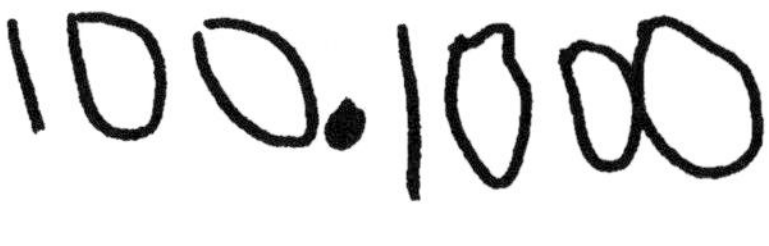

Figure 4.4. Thomas's writing of 100,000.

as "one thousand." In this way, the period helps the reader—Thomas—decide how to read the digits placed before the punctuation mark: 10.000 is "*ten* thousand," 1.000 is "*one*." The period also helps the reader decide how to read the digits placed after the punctuation mark: digits placed after periods are either not read (as in 1.000 read as "one"), or they are read in a different way (as in 9.91, where the digits after the period mean cents instead of dollars).

During our third interview, Thomas elaborated on an interesting idea regarding what "periods" in numbers are for. At one point during the interview, he suggested using no periods for writing the number 1,000,000,000, and then exclaimed, "If there are no periods . . . but they don't *do* anything!" I asked Thomas what periods were for then, and he explained, "The period just tells you to stop. . . . It's like a red light. It tells you to stop and read that." In this explanation, Thomas was making explicit the understanding he had been acting on during the previous two sessions of work. When he said, "It tells you to stop and read that," Thomas meant that the period in 10,000 (i.e., 10.000 [see Figure 4.3]), for example, told you to read the first part, "ten," and then stop. After stopping, you could read or decide what to do with the rest of the number. Another example of Thomas's use of punctuation marks to aid in the reading of numbers was provided in the fourth interview. In that session, Thomas wrote the number "seven thousand and forty" as 7040. Since at this point in our work together, Thomas had started using commas in his writing of numbers, I asked him if he could put a comma in the number he had just written. Thomas wrote 70,40, while I simultaneously wrote 7,040. When I noticed the difference between our two notations, I showed it to Thomas and asked him what he thought. He said that 70,40 said "*seventy* thousand and forty"—apparently using his rule of stopping and reading after the punctuation mark—and that "*seven* thousand and forty" was 7,040. So he changed the comma in his notation and wrote 7,040.

During our second session of work together, Thomas began to explore ideas about how a number would change if it had a period or comma in it, and if it didn't. For example, when I presented Thomas with the two numbers 1000 and 1.000, Thomas explained to me that the two numbers were not the same number. The first number was "one thousand" and the second was "one," because "the zeros after the period don't count"; he was rejecting the possibility that "one thousand" could be written with a period in it. In subsequent sessions, Thomas also struggled with deciding whether two numbers that had the same digits, one of them having a period or comma in it and the second not, could be the same number. For example, during our fourth interview, Thomas struggled with deciding whether numbers with and without periods such as 1000 and 1.000, or numbers with and without commas such as 10000 and 10,000, were the same numbers or not. By the end of this fourth session, Thomas accepted that 1000 and 1,000 could be the same number ("one thousand") but did not make the same judgment regarding 10000 and 10,000—these were two different numbers. He interpreted the first number as "one million" and the second as "ten thousand." Possibly, the lack of punctuation marks in 10000 led him to just see many zeros, as in "one million." Given that by the end of our work together, Thomas quite consistently used commas and periods when writing numbers, he was less likely to have to make decisions about numbers without punctuation marks in them. It is possible that Thomas's gradually more consistent use of punctuation marks in numbers helped him to deal with this problem.

Toward the end of our fourth session of work, Thomas began to reject the use of periods, and instead accepted commas in numbers such as 1,410 (read by him as "one thousand four hundred and ten"), 7,040 ("seven thousand forty"), 10,000 ("ten thousand"), and 300,010 ("three hundred thousand and ten"). Thomas explained to me that periods and commas were different, although he wasn't sure how. While "the period tells you to stop," he didn't know what the comma did. Throughout the fifth session of work, Thomas continued to use commas when writing and interpreting numbers, as in 10,000 ("ten thousand"), 54,005 ("fifty four thousand and five"), and 700,001 ("seven hundred thousand and one"). In addition, by the sixth interview, Thomas began to use periods and commas interchangeably. He went from the exclusive use of periods, to the exclusive use of commas, to the possible use of both. By our final session together, Thomas consistently used "commas and periods" interchangeably, although he explained that they were still slightly different: The period lets you know where to stop and read, while the comma "is probably just a pause . . . but I don't know if it's really for pausing." In spite of this, when writing numbers, Thomas had begun to use commas almost exclusively (as when writing 10,000, 100,000 and 1,000,000). But when interpreting numbers, he took periods and commas to be the same (so that 1.000 and 1,000 were "one thousand" and 10.000 and 10,000 were "ten thousand").

Thomas's interpretations and understandings about the use and role of periods and commas in numbers might be similar to his developing understandings in the area of written language. That periods "tell you to stop" and that commas "tell you to pause" sounds vaguely familiar. This possible "similarity," however, does not in any way imply that Thomas could not distinguish between written language and numerical notations. Because he was learning both notation systems simultaneously, his understandings in each area might naturally overlap and extend into the other area. We might even wonder, in the history of numerical notations, how it came to be that periods and commas began to be used. We will explore this in the following sections. For now, it is interesting to note that punctuation marks had similar uses in the early history of musical notation and in written language to those described by Thomas for numerical notation (see Treitler, 1982).

The Use of Periods and Commas to Organize Numbers Graphically

In addition to using punctuation marks as aids for his reading of numbers, Thomas began to gradually use periods and commas to provide some kind of *graphic organization* for numbers. The use of the punctuation marks for reading and for organizing the numbers graphically are not disassociated, as we will see. In fact, the consistent graphic organization of the numbers through the use of periods and commas was an aid in Thomas's reading of the numbers.

During our first two sessions of work together, Thomas made explicit some of his understandings regarding the graphic organization of numbers. It was not obvious to me that this was what he was doing, however, until one of our later sessions. For instance, he began reading groups of two zeros as "hundred." In this way, Thomas read the number 10.00 as "ten hundred." Groups of two zeros were "hundred," probably because the number 100 contains two zeros. In addition, groups of two or three zeros—the "batches of zeros," as he came to call them—were divided by periods, and the periods told you how to read those batches. A batch of two zeros, for example, was interpreted as "hundred," while a batch of three zeros was interpreted as "thousand." Three zeros were called "thousand" probably because of the fact that the number 1,000 has three zeros in it.

Further examples of Thomas's use of punctuation marks to organize numbers were provided during our fourth session of work together. During that session, Thomas was very consistent in his use of the periods, and later of commas, using them to divide the numbers into groups ("batches") of three digits. For instance, when Thomas wrote "seven thousand and forty" as 7040 and decided to place a comma after the first two digits (i.e., 70,40), he then changed his mind and turned the number into 7,040. He insisted that if the number was going to be "*seven* thousand" as opposed to "*seventy* thousand," then the comma had to be placed in that position. This is an example of Thomas's simultaneous use of punctuation marks for *reading* numbers and for *organizing* them graphically into "batches" of two or three digits.

During the fourth session, Thomas began to speak of the batches of zeros that numbers have in them. He referred to the batches as being groups of three digits. For example, when he compared my writing of "one billion" (1,000,000,000) with his writing of "five million" (5000,000,000), Thomas told me that the number *I* had written was "one *million*," because "it's missing one more batch of zeros." This was a very graphic way to group the digits and referred once again to how he used the punctuation marks to organize the numbers. Thomas told me that "million" had three batches of zeros and so "billion" had to have one more batch of zeros than "million." In his mind, "one billion" should be written as 1,000,000,000,000.

Further, during our fifth interview, when Thomas first set out to write the number "ten thousand," he wrote 10 000, leaving a space in between the first two digits and the rest. Cajori (1928) notes that in 1540, the mathematician Gemma Frisius left spaces between groups of three digits. Thomas explained to me that he left a space after 10, "instead of a comma." In this exchange, Thomas was also trying to organize the number graphically, in some way.

Then, during our following interview, Thomas was ordering a collection of cards, from the numbers that were least to the numbers that were more. He had a card with 10.00 written on it. When it came time to decide where to put it within the serial ordering, he said: "It's ten hundred . . . this [pointing to 10.00] is one thousand, 'cause there is no such thing as ten hundred, so it has to be one thousand." Thomas was using the period to tell him how to *read* the number. He was also thinking about groups of two zeros as representing "hundred." In this instance, Thomas's approach of using periods to read numbers conflicted with his newly developed method of organizing numbers graphically into batches of three digits. As written, the number should be "ten hundred." But because of the batches of zeros it had, it should really be "one thousand." However, "one thousand" is actually the *same* as "ten hundreds," in terms of quantity, if we rearrange the batches in the number. Thomas's understandings based on the use of the periods in numbers and on batches of digits will need to be coordinated with another aspect of the written number system, place value. Once Thomas's current understandings are connected to place value, he may not find them as conflicting but as two instantiations of different aspects of the written number system. In this way, he may be able to see 10.00 both as "ten hundreds" and as "one thousand," the conventional reading being "one thousand."

Thomas's reading of 10.00 as necessarily being "one thousand" can also be taken as an example of his need to adjust to the conventions for reading and writing numbers. We can imagine that at some point in his development, Thomas could accept for "one thousand" to be rearranged into 10 hundreds, making it possible for him to read 10.00 as "ten hundred." Although 10.00 should be "ten hundred" following his rule about the use of periods in numbers as telling you where to stop and read, he had never heard of this reading before, and he therefore used the batches of zeros to let him know that this number was "one thousand."

In the same interview, wondering whether Thomas might think of 10.00 as being "dollars and cents" once again, as he had interpreted 9.91 (see Figure 4.1) to be during our first interview, I posed a question.

BÁRBARA: What else can it [i.e., 10.00] be?
THOMAS: Ten hundred, but there is no such thing as ten hundred so it's one thousand.
BÁRBARA: Are there any other numbers that have two numbers at the end like that?
THOMAS: No, I don't think so.

I wanted to make sure that he considered the possibility of 10.00 being money, as he had assumed 9.91 to be earlier.

BÁRBARA: Do you think that this [number] (pointing to 10.00) could be ten dollars and zero cents?
THOMAS: It *can* be, but it's not money, so it *can't* be.

So, Thomas continued to think of 10.00 as "one thousand." In this excerpt, Thomas was thinking about how many zeros numbers have—how many batches of zeros—in deciding which number it was. He was switching between using the period to help him in reading the number, to using the period to organize the number into batches, and finally to trying to constrain himself to using batches of three digits. Continuing to order the numbers he had written on cards, Thomas placed 1.000 and 1000 together, as being the same number. He also wanted to place 10.00 together with these numbers, and I began to ask him how he was deciding that it was "one thousand." In trying to adjust to this question, Thomas said, "Let's just add one zero . . . so we know that . . . no, I think that's bad . . . if we make another zero it would be ten thousand, not one thousand. We have to cross this out [the zero in between the one and the period] to make it one thousand [and then adding a zero at the end of the number]." So Thomas ended up writing 10.000, crossing out the zero before the period and adding one zero at the end. He said that now the number was certainly "one thousand." He said, "If you put one zero only here [at the end of the number] it would be *ten* thousand, so you have to cross out the zero here [the zero before the period] [to have one thousand]." This was an instance when Thomas was trying to combine the use of the periods and commas for *reading* numbers with his new idea about batches of zeros and his use of punctuation marks to *organize numbers graphically.*

While during the previous session Thomas had decided that 1,000,000 should be interpreted as "three more zeros than one thousand," during this session he began to call this number "one thousand thousand." Again, "one million" is "one thousand thousand," if we think in terms of quantity.

Then, during the seventh session of work together, Thomas decided to add a comma to his number 10000, which he had interpreted as being "one million" during our first session together, to make it "ten thousand": 10,000. Because Thomas had earlier confidently interpreted 10,000 as "ten thousand," I asked him about adding a comma.

> BÁRBARA: If you had to put a comma [in 10000], where would you put it?
> THOMAS: Right here [adding a comma to 10000 and making it 10,000]. But then it would have to [be] ten thousand.

Again, Thomas was using the punctuation mark—the comma, in this case—to organize the number into batches of three digits, and to read the number. During our last interview, when I wrote the number 10,0000, Thomas looked at it and first counted the number of zeros, added a zero in between the first and second zero from the left, and then moved the comma. He ended up with 1000,000. Thomas said that this number was "one thousand thousand" but that he could change it into "one million" by adding one more comma, ending up with 1,000,000. By the end of this session, Thomas wrote the number 5,000,000 and interpreted it as "five million," and then wrote 4,000,000,000 and interpreted it as "four thousand million." These are other examples of Thomas's use of the punctuation marks to organize the numbers into batches of three digits. Although Thomas was not always using the conventional names for the numbers, he was still being consistent in his naming of the numbers, focusing on the progressions in the "batches of zeros."

REFLECTIONS

In Thomas's interview, it is relevant to highlight the truly constructive nature of the learning that he engaged in. While his object of study was figurative in nature, his learning of it was operative or constructive. Further, it is also important to highlight the similarities between Thomas's thinking about periods and commas in numbers and some of the landmarks in the history of notations of social use—such as numerical notations, musical notations, and written language. The similarities have to do with the types of mechanisms of thought and cognitive obstacles that can be identified in the development of numerical notations (see Ferreiro, 1991; Ferreiro & Teberosky, 1979). These similarities, however, do not imply, in any way, a causal relationship between the history of notations of social use and Thomas's thinking about the use of periods and commas in numbers.

As with Thomas, there were two distinct uses for punctuation marks in the history of numerical notations: to group digits in numeration (as in his batches of zeros) and for marking the whole and decimal parts of numbers (Cajori, 1928). Cajori explains that "in the writing of numbers containing many digits it is desirable to have some symbol separating the numbers into groups of, say, three digits" (p. 57). The various symbols used throughout the history of numerical notations that organize numbers into groups of digits have been, most frequently, periods, commas, dots, vertical bars, arcs, colons, and semicolons. Thus, Thomas's switching from the use of periods to the use of commas is paralleled in the observations made throughout the history of numerical notations.

Texts on the history of numerical notations rarely contain reflections on the types of cognitive obstacles that were encountered and that eventually led to the use of punctuation marks in numbers. However, if we maintain the assumption that the uses and interpretations that Thomas was making of punctuation marks in numbers were similar to their uses in written language, we might turn to contemporary and historical reflections on the use of punctuation marks in written language. The reflections on the origins of these graphic marks in the area of written language are interesting in light of Thomas's developing understandings. For example, Ferreiro (Ferreiro & Zucchermaglio, 1996; Ferreiro, Pontecorvo, Ribeiro Moreira, & García Hidalgo, 1996) notes how there exists a theory of punctuation as a natural "breathing place" for readers, that pervades both schools and the history of written language. In fact, Parkes (1992) has called this a "grammar of legibility." Punctuation marks aid readers; in fact, the use of punctuation marks originated in readers—not writers—to guide interpretation (Parkes, 1992; see Ferreiro, Pontecorvo, Ribeiro Moreira, & García Hidalgo, 1996). As Parkes (1978) explains, punctuation marks helped a reader make sense of a text, by marking off the sense units of the text.

Ferreiro points to the use of punctuation marks throughout the evolution of writing both as organizers of texts and as a way to limit readers' interpretations (Ferreiro, Pontecorvo, Ribeiro Moreira, & García Hidalgo, 1996). This is very similar to the kinds of uses that Thomas makes of punctuation marks in numbers: to aid in his reading of numbers and to organize numbers graphically. In Thomas, this latter organization tends gradually to the grouping of three digits into batches.

An exploration of some instances in the history of musical notations in the West reveals the parallels with written language in the use of punctuation marks. It therefore also points to parallels between Thomas's understandings of punctuation marks in numbers and their use in written language and in musical notation. For example, a writer of about the year 1100 explains:

> Just as in prose three kinds of *distinctiones* are recognized, which can also be called "pauses"—namely, the colon, that is, member; the comma or *incisio*; and the period, *clausula* or *circuitus*—so also it is in chant. In prose, where one makes a pause in reading aloud, this is called a colon; when the sentence is divided by an appropriate punctuation mark, it is called a comma; when the sentence is brought to an end, it is a period.
>
> Likewise, when a chant makes a pause by dwelling on the fourth or fifth note above the final, there is a colon; when in mid-course it returns to the final, there is a comma; when it arrives at the final at the end, there is a period. (Johannes, quoted in Treitler, 1982, pp. 269–270)

While there are similarities between the use of punctuation marks in written language and in Thomas's use of punctuation marks, there are parallel similarities between the use of punctuation marks in written language and in the history of musical notations. Further, Treitler (1982) notes that "[musical] notational signs and punctuation marks therefore play a similar role in guiding the singer/reader in bringing out the sense of a text" (p. 270). What I would like to point to are the similarities between the uses and interpretations of punctuation marks in numbers by Thomas and their uses and interpretations in other notation systems of social use such as written language and musical notations. I do not think we have enough evidence, however, to describe or say in which notation system the use of punctuation marks first originated and into which system they were adopted. As Treitler (1982) points out:

> Whether these signs and their functions were developed for one practice and borrowed for the other, and if so, what the direction of borrowing was, are questions we cannot yet answer. The main point for the moment is to establish that there *is* this common aspect to musical notation and punctuation. (p. 271)

Once again, while Thomas's object of study was figurative in nature, his learning of it was operative or constructive. Hence, I am arguing that there can be an operative and constructive process involved in the appropriation of an object of knowledge that is imminently figurative, like the written number system. Furthermore, throughout the eight sessions that Thomas and I spent together, one might argue, the periods and commas in numbers became conceptual objects for Thomas.

I also hope to have offered, through this account, a reflection on the need for further studies that describe the type of operative and constructive work involved in children's learning of the written number system. There is a need for studies that explore the logic and hypotheses of children as they reinvent the written number system. Children develop systematic ideas about the written number system. Through the excerpts presented here, I also meant to show the need to give a place to the written number system in the realm of the genesis of mathematical knowledge. I continue to argue that children don't first develop their ideas about the conceptual aspects of numbers, and later on engage in understanding and learning about the written aspects of numbers. Further, children do not begin their formal instruction in numbers as a tabula rasa regarding their knowledge about written numbers.

Sara: Notations for Fractions That Help Her "Think of Something"

With Analúcia Schliemann and David Carraher

> DAVID (seeing Sara's pie charts for representing thirds): And should . . . are these pieces [the thirds] the same size, or are they different sizes?
>
> SARA: Well, I don't, when I draw this, it's just to help me think of something, so it doesn't really matter.
>
> DAVID: It doesn't really matter. But if you drew it perfectly, should you draw them the same size or different sizes? Or doesn't it matter?
>
> SARA: The same size.
>
> DAVID: Oh, OK.

In the previous chapters I have focused on children's understanding of different aspects of the written number system. Mathematical notations, however, are not constrained to representing the number system. This chapter and those that follow will focus on other kinds of notations, such as those for fractions, data tables, and Cartesian coordinate graphs, used mostly in the context of solving algebraic-type problems.

The focus of this chapter is a third grader named Sara. Sara exemplifies, through her actions and her words, how notations can represent not only what was done in the process of solving a problem but also how notations can become tools for *thinking and reflecting about a problem*. Sara's example helps us to begin to think about children's notations not only as tools with which learners can represent their understanding and thinking, but also as tools to *further* those understandings and that thinking. As Sara explained during an interview, referring to the pie chart she had drawn to represent the fractions she was thinking about, "Well, I don't . . . when I draw this [the pie chart] it's just to help me think of something, so it doesn't really matter [if the pieces of the pie chart are different sizes]."

The work with Sara was undertaken as part of an Early Algebra study with a classroom of 18 third-grade students at a public elementary school during a one-year teaching experiment. Chapters 6 and 7 describe a continuation of this Early Algebra project into a longitudinal study in the same school setting. The school in which we worked serves a diverse multiethnic and racial community that is reflected well in the classroom composition, which included children from South America, Asia, Europe, and North America. The school population was 75% Latino, and 83.09% of the children were eligible for free or reduced-price lunch.

The work had been undertaken to understand and document issues of learning and teaching in an "algebrafied" (Kaput, 1995) or "algebratized" (Davydov, 1991) arithmetical setting. The instruction activities in the classroom consisted of teaching a 2-hour "math class" on a biweekly basis. The topics for the class sessions evolved from a combination of the curriculum content, the teacher's main goals for each semester, and the questions we brought to the table. During the teaching experiments, notations were an integral part of the work with the children.

In this chapter, the specific content Sara deals with is that of fractions, in the context of algebraic-type problems. Researchers have increasingly come to conclude that young children can understand mathematical concepts assumed to be fundamental to learning algebra (Brito-Lima & da Rocha Falcão, 1997; Carraher, Schliemann, & Brizuela, 1999; Schifter, 1998; Schliemann, Carraher, Pendexter, & Brizuela, 1998). Many researchers and educators now believe that elementary algebraic ideas and notation are an integral part of young students' understanding of early mathematics. Children's *algebraic reasoning* refers to cases in which they express general properties of numbers (e.g., "whenever you divide by 2 a number that ends in an even digit, the remainder will be zero") or quantities (e.g., "regardless of how much candy John has, if he has two thirds as much candy as Mark, then Mark has one and one half times as much candy as John does"). Although children can spontaneously express such general properties and relations through natural language, without making use of other notations, they can also express these properties and relations through written notation, without having to treat conventional notation as a mere appendage to reasoning. It thereby becomes necessary to document how children's symbolic repertoire for expressing general properties gradually expands. Children do not move suddenly from symbol-free expression to conventional written notation. Words are symbols. Diagrams are symbols. Written mathematical notation is symbolic whether or not it conforms to mathematical convention. The task before us is to document how children initially express general relations and gradually assimilate conventional notations into their expressive repertoire. It thus becomes crucial to ask ourselves how the child's reasoning itself evolves and to wonder what role, if any, the newly assimilated symbolic notations play in the course of this evolution of thinking. These issues are aligned with a question posed by Kaput (1991): "How do material notations and mental constructions interact to produce new constructions?" (p. 55).

In previous analyses of young children's use of notations in problems requiring algebraic reasoning, we identified the gradual way in which children's notations became more and more context independent (Brizuela, Carraher, & Schliemann, 2000). At the beginning of the school year, the notations that children created to represent and solve algebraic problems were imbued with features peculiar to the problem at hand. For example, in representing a problem in which 17 fish had been reduced to 11 fish, children drew fish, with eyes, tails, and fins. While these notations served well the purpose of representing the problem at hand, they would probably not serve well the task of representing problems with a similar underlying structure, such as representing how a bank balance of 17 dollars fell to 11 dollars. As the weeks went by, however, the children's notations became more schematic and general, focusing on the logical relationships between quantities instead of the physical properties of the quantities themselves. To further explore children's notations in early algebra, we began to consider the role that the notations may play in the children's thinking about different problems.

An essential part of children's mathematical development is their understanding of fractions (see, for example, the NCTM 2002 yearbook dedicated to this topic, in Litwiller, 2002). Children's experience with fractions begins even before formal schooling (Smith, 2002). Likewise, children's self-developed symbols and notations for fractions are crucial to the children's conceptual understanding. As is the case in other areas of mathematics, in the domain of fractions, "children's uses of pictures enable them to understand and resolve situations and perform procedures they might otherwise find beyond their grasp" (Sharp, Garofalo, & Adams, 2002, p. 27). Empson (2002) has also highlighted that, in the area of fractions, "representational tools . . . are the means to solve problems and express thinking" (p. 35).

In his work regarding cultural tools and mathematical learning, Cobb (1995) highlights two opposing perspectives—the sociocultural and the constructivist—in the analysis of children's notations. One could argue from a sociocultural perspective that children internalize the notations used by the mathematical community. One could also argue, presumably from a constructivist perspective, that conceptual development will occur independently of the cultural tools, such as notation, that members of the learners' community make use of. The position taken in this chapter is midway between these views. That is, the task is to explore and document how the assimilation of conventional notation interacts with children's conceptual development.

In this chapter, we will also briefly explore the connections and possible similarities between the notations developed by children and some of the landmarks in the history of mathematical notations. Charles Babbage, for example, writing in 1827 about the advantages inherent in the invention of algebraic notation, stated:

> The quantity of meaning compressed into small space by algebraic signs, is another circumstance that facilitates the reasonings we are accustomed to carry on by their aid. The assumption of lines and figures to represent quantity and magnitude, was the method employed by the ancient geometers to present to the eye some picture by which the course of their reasonings might be traced: it was however necessary to fill up this outline by a tedious description, which in some instances even of no peculiar difficulty became nearly unintelligible, simply from its extreme length: the invention of algebra almost entirely removed this inconvenience. (In Cajori, 1929, p. 331)

In this case, we will need to explore, in the notations of Sara and the third graders we worked with, whether their notations of the problems help them to compress the meaning they made of the problems. A. N. Whitehead referred bluntly to this process in 1911: "By relieving the brain of all unnecessary work, a good notation sets it free to concentrate on more advanced problems" (in Cajori, 1929, p. 332). What effects might the use of written notations while solving algebraic problems have on children's reasoning processes?

SOLVING ALGEBRAIC PROBLEMS DURING CLASS

At our May 28 class, which was the 15th and final class meeting with us, David Carraher (who was the instructor for this teaching experiment) and our third-grade students were solving fraction problems. The first problem presented to the class to think about was the following:

> Jessica spent one third of her money to buy ice cream.
> After buying the ice cream, she ended up with $6.
> How much money did she start with?
> How do you know?
>
> Draw a picture showing:

Her money before buying ice cream.
The money she spent for the ice cream.
The money she had after buying the ice cream.

As we had done many times before, we encouraged the students to use any kind of notation they felt comfortable with—arrows, shapes, drawings, or pie charts. The children had been introduced to the use of pie charts as notations for unit fractions by their regular classroom teacher in the week preceding this class. As the students began to think about the preceding problem, Jenny proposed that the answer should be 24—in other words, that Jessica must have started with $24. Explaining her solution by referring to fourths rather than thirds, she explained, "One fourth of it [the money she had] is $6, if you add $6 four times it should be 24." Following this, David asked for more volunteers:

DAVID: Does anybody else have another analysis to give us?
NATHIA: What is analysis?
DAVID: (Sara put her hand up to participate) OK. Sara, go ahead, show us what you're understanding.
SARA: She (referring to Jenny) said one fourth. But it [the problem] says one third. So you kind of draw it into parts like this, I mean like that (drawing a pie chart into thirds, with a number 6 written in each section of the pie).
DAVID: How many parts do you have there?
SARA: Three.
MICHAEL: (Referring to the pie chart cut into thirds) That's a peace sign.
SARA: Six, six, and six (pointing to the three "pie pieces" in her diagram). So six and six is twelve (pointing to two pieces of her pie chart). And six is $18 all together (pointing to the last piece).
DAVID: So now we have two different answers [for the total amount of money Jessica had—24 and 18]. Go ahead.
SARA: (Reading the problem) One third of her money on ice cream. And . . . but . . . I did that wrong (going back to her notation of the pie chart).
DAVID: You did that wrong, why?
SARA: Because it should be like this (crossing out her first notation and then drawing a pie chart into thirds, this time with number 3 written in each section). Because if she has $9, this is her ice cream (pointing to one of the pieces), and then this is the $6 that she ended up with (pointing to the two remaining pieces and referring to the $6 mentioned in the problem). If she spent

this (pointing to one piece) for her ice cream, there's three and
three (pointing to the two pieces of the pie chart that remained).

DAVID: So now you're thinking she might have had $9 instead of
   18. OK.

In this example, we see Sara trying to figure out the problem she was presented with, and using the notations she makes to help her figure out her
answer. Figure 5.1 shows the notations that Sara made that day in class,
on her paper, for this problem, after having solved it in front of the whole
class.

While trying to solve the problem in front of the whole class, Sara first
represented her thinking about the problem—what she thought the problem was stating. She did not attempt to represent all the *actions* that took
place in the problem—such as the buying of the ice cream and the spending
of the money—but instead extracted the essential information to enable
her to solve the problem. Sara's writing "left" and "ice cream" could be
taken to represent the different actions in the problem. These particular
notations, however, were not made *while* she was solving the problem, and
seem to express the "types" of quantities (i.e., this is the money that was
left over or the money that was spent) more than the different steps of the
problem.

The first issue to sort out in this problem was that of "the thirds"—
especially given that the problem had first been presented in terms of
fourths by Jenny, a very important class participant. Then, as Sara used
the notation as a tool with which to reflect on the problem once again, she
was able to return to the problem and think about it through the lens that
she had created with her notation. In returning and reflecting, she *changed*
her thinking. Sara found that the first pie chart that she had made, with 6,
6, and 6, did not correspond to having two thirds of the amount being six,
as had been mentioned in the problem. So using this first notation as a
springboard, she only had to make a minor adjustment for her initial nota-

Figure 5.1. Sara's notations for solving the ice cream problem.

tion to match what was going on in the problem. Although Sara was using the type of notation for fractions preferred in the context of her classroom (i.e., the pie chart), she was still appropriating this particular notation and making use of it to figure out the problem—in a way, we may say that she was reinventing the notation. In fact, we found that the use of the pie charts to represent unit fractions did not necessarily help the children to solve or understand the different fraction problems. We are reminded here of E. Mach's point, made in 1906, that "symbols which initially appear to have no meaning whatever, acquire gradually, after subjection to what might be called intellectual experimenting, a lucid and precise significance" (in Cajori, 1929, p. 330). Symbols, such as the "pie chart," don't automatically lead to an understanding about fractions.

The following episode, from later during that same class, illustrates once again how Sara was using the notations to think and reflect about the problem. The children had begun to work individually or in pairs on a second problem:

> Claudia decided to buy a book about lizards.
> Yesterday she had only one fourth of the money she needed to buy the book.
> Today Claudia earned $3.00 more.
> Now she has one half of the money she needs.
>
> How much does the book cost?
>
> Draw a picture showing:
> How much money she had yesterday.
> How much money she needs.
>
> Try to show where the $3.00 fits in your picture.

David Carraher noticed Sara's solution to the problem and called Analúcia Schliemann over so Sara could explain her notations and her thinking:

> I decided that . . . Claudia decided to buy a book about lizards. Yesterday she had only one fourth of the money she needs to buy the book (reading the problem). When it said one fourth I decided I'd draw the circle with the line and the line (referring to the pie chart and the vertical and horizontal lines cutting through it [Figure 5.2a]). And then Claudia earned three more (continuing to read the prob-

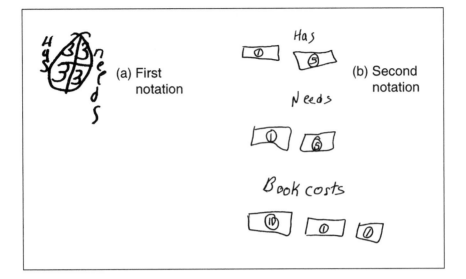

Figure 5.2. Sara's notations for the Claudia problem.

lem). I figured, she probably had three dollars before and then she earned three more. So I put the three down there and the three down there (pointing to the two 3s on the lower half of the pie chart). But if you go like this, that's a half and that's a half (pointing to each of the halves in the pie chart), so she has a half and she needs a half, so the book costs $12.

Although Sara was not followed *while* she was solving the problem, she was able to verbalize, in considerable detail, the process she went through and how she used the notations to solve the problem. The notation she made helped her, first, to structure her thinking about the problem. When the problem stated that Claudia had one fourth, then earned three more, and finally had one half of the money she needed, she used the information in the problem to assume—correctly—that each fourth had to be the same. In this case, each fourth of the money had to be $3. The fact that Sara chose the number 3 *might* have been fortuitous; she may have fallen on this number and it happened to work. But this was probably not the case, because the notation that she developed from that inference was based on her thinking about fractions and it also helped to expand it.

Later that same day, Sara, encouraged by David, made a statement about the use of different types of notations that is very relevant to the topic being addressed in this chapter. Working on the problem about Claudia, Sara proposed two different notations. First, she made the notation that she had described for Analúcia in front of the whole class and explained it. Then, she made a second notation, saying, "I have another way that isn't using a pie." Figure 5.2b shows the notation that she made, representing the dollar bills that Claudia would need to buy her book. When she completed this notation, David spoke to her.

> DAVID: You know, Sara, I think one of the . . . you do two different drawings. One is a good drawing if you haven't figured it out yet, and another one is a drawing that works if, only if you know, if you've already figured it out.
>
> SARA: Yeah, if you've already figured it [the problem] out this one is good (pointing to Figure 5.2b), but if you haven't, the pie one would probably be better (see Figure 5.2a). If like someone already did the pie and you want to show it differently, you might want to use this one (pointing to Figure 5.2b).

As she explained, one of these notations, namely, the pie chart, helped her to *think* about the problem, while the other, the currency notation, just showed what she did *after solving* the problem. But we might want to argue that while the pie chart notation helped her to *structure* her thinking, she then also used it to *restructure* it: She reorganized the amounts ($3 + 3 = 5 + 1$; and $12 = 10 + 1 + 1$) into relationships that referred to what Claudia had, what Claudia needed, and the total cost of the book, as well as reorganizing the amounts (from \$1 and \$5 to \$10, \$1, and \$1).

SOLVING ALGEBRAIC PROBLEMS DURING AN INTERVIEW

In June, after 15 classroom meetings that were held throughout the school year, we had individual interviews with some of the children in the group. David interviewed Sara and Parabdeep about the following fraction problem, a follow-up of our last class in May:

Two thirds of a fish weighs 10 pounds.
How heavy is the whole fish?

First, Sara read the problem. Immediately after doing so, she proposed a solution.

SARA: Twenty pounds. Because, two thirds . . . no, wait, 15 pounds.
'Cause it would be like (drawing a crude pie chart of thirds [Figure 5.3a]), five, ten, fifteen (pointing to each one of the thirds).

DAVID: My goodness.

SARA: And there's ten (pointing to two of the thirds), and there's five (pointing to the third third).

DAVID: So what is the . . . you drew this drawing so quickly! Parabdeep, she didn't even give us a chance to think about it, did she? Sara, what does this mean? . . . Let's read that again. Two thirds of a fish weighs 10 pounds.

SARA: I thought, I was trying to, because at first I thought it was like that (drawing a pie chart of fourths [Figure 5.3b]) but then I remembered that it was this (referring to the thirds in Figure 5.3a). So I figured it can't be that [fourths], it had to be this [thirds].

DAVID: Did you draw thirds or fourths here? (Referring to Figure 5.3b)

(a) Thirds   (b) Fourths

(c) A "correct" notation for thirds

Figure 5.3. Sara's notations for the fish fraction problem.

SARA: That was in fourths. I thought, I'm like "two" (referring to the mention of "two thirds" in the problem), and I jumped and I thought it was four.

DAVID: So now you did it this way? (referring to Figure 5.3a)

SARA: Yeah.

DAVID: And actually you changed very quickly. And should . . . are these pieces the same size, or are they different sizes (referring to the thirds segments in Figure 5.3a)?

SARA: Well, I don't, *when I draw this it's just to help me think of something, so it doesn't really matter* (emphasis added).

DAVID: It doesn't really matter. But if you drew it perfectly, should you draw them the same size or different sizes? Or doesn't it matter?

SARA: The same size.

DAVID: Oh, OK.

SARA: So, if I wanted to draw it right, it would probably look like, maybe like that (drawing an accurately proportioned pie chart of thirds [Figure 5.3c]).

Here, Sara is clearly stating that she is using the notation to help her think. The notation is helping her go through the problem and is helpful in allowing her to reflect on the problem. Even the notation that she has not yet made, but is still thinking about, helps her to reflect on the problem. The notation comes to be a sort of "mental image" (Piaget & Inhelder, 1966/1971) for her understanding of the problem. Objectifying and reifying this mental image (Piaget, 1974/1976; Piaget & García, 1982), she was able to reflect on it, to clarify and further her thinking about the problem.

REFLECTIONS

Like Cobb's students using the hundreds board (Cobb, 1995), one cannot argue that Sara *understood* the fraction problems because she had access to the "pie chart" notation. The evidence, furthermore, is not conclusive. For example, there is no evidence for how her thinking about fractions and her notations for them evolved. What we do have is a small snapshot of the process she went through in solving a series of problems about fractions, and hypotheses about the role that the notations might have played. In addition, one can say that her notations helped her to reflect on the problems and to further her understanding of the problem. The notations Sara made helped her to think about the problems, and in that thinking—and reflecting—process, her understanding became more complex.

Sara's initial challenge was to find a notation that would adequately help her to *think about* the problems at hand. As she herself explained, the pie chart helped her to think about the Claudia problem, while the dollar-bill notation (not one of the "tools" that had been presented to her in class) did not (see Figures 5.2a and b). Similar to Babbage's reflection (see Cajori, 1929) about the advantages of algebraic notation, Sara's reasonings were facilitated by the pie charts she made—diagrams that did not, however, describe in detail all that happened in the problem. By compressing meaning into her notations, Sara was able to reason about the problem, using the notation itself as a springboard and a tool for developing that reasoning.

Furthermore, one could venture to argue that Sara's notations supported and furthered her algebraic reasoning. Her notations represented general relations between quantities. In fact, the notations she made for the ice cream problem (see Figure 5.1), for the Claudia problem (see Figure 5.2), and for the fish-weight problem (see Figure 5.3) could actually stand for any other problem that referred to the same quantities. The notations do not express the actions that took place in the problem, or the operations that were carried out with the quantities, but the general relations between the quantities in the problem. The notations she made helped her to change her thinking and to reflect on the problems presented to her.

Referring back to Kaput's (1991) question "How do material notations and mental constructions interact to produce new constructions?" (p. 55), one could begin by saying that although Sara's notations are not conventional algebraic notations, they do constitute an internalization of a conventional notation accepted within the context of her class, and the gradual appropriation of that notation to allow her to support and further her algebraic reasoning. That is, this is a midpoint between the dichotomous views presented at the outset of this chapter by Cobb (1995)—the sociocultural and the constructivist.

Jennifer and Her Peers: Data Tables and Additive Relations

With Susanna Lara-Roth

> JENNIFER: [A real math table] shows how they did, like uh, like shows how much they have and you could compare them. . . . Like, they both have seven, they both have twelve, and then, she has four more.
>
> BÁRBARA: OK. So what do you think that tables are used for in math?
>
> JENNIFER: To compare . . . You could use them for comparing, and you could use them for also to do the math.

Jennifer is a third grader with whom we worked in the context of an Early Algebra study, which was an extension of the study that Sara (see Chapter 5) had participated in. We worked with Jennifer and her peers from the second semester of second grade through fourth grade, teaching in their math classes for an average of eight lessons each semester. During our work with these children in second and third grade, we covered the following topics: "more" and "less"; additive comparisons; addition and subtraction as functions; generalized numbers and variables; multiplication and division; graphs and number lines; tables for organizing information and looking at functions; and conventional notations, including algebraic inscriptions. In our work with these elementary school students we placed an emphasis on notations for algebraic problems. One of the types of notations that became important was that of data tables.

Although tables are an integral part of the mathematics curriculum, we know surprisingly little about how this tool lends itself to the understanding of algebra and in particular to the understanding of functions.

Specifically, we do not know how children's understanding of tables as a notational tool relates to their parallel, evolving understanding of algebra and functions. The same cannot be said of other tools related to functions, such as graphs, where there has been considerable research describing children's understanding and construction of them (e.g., diSessa et al., 1991; Leinhardt, Zaslavsky, & Stein, 1990; Nemirovsky, Tierney, & Wright, 1998; Tierney & Nemirovsky, 1995), or other types of diagrams (e.g., Sellke, Behr, & Voelker, 1991; Simon & Stimpson, 1988). In this chapter, we address several questions: What is the nature of children's understanding of tables? How does their understanding evolve? What do children learn about functions, about algebra, and about mathematics when working with tables? And what issues might educators and curriculum developers need to take into account when designing learning activities that employ tables?

The work we present in this chapter stands in contrast with research carried out up to now. Sellke and his colleagues view the use of "linking tables" or diagrams as

> overrid[ing] the influence of the intuitive models and the numerical constraints associated with them, overrid[ing] the inaccurate conceptions many students have of the two operations, reflect[ing] multiplicative relationships between the quantities, remain[ing] true to the semantic meaning of the problem, and [being] effective regardless of the numerical characteristics. (Sellke et al., 1991, p. 31)

Simon and Stimpson (1988) suggest that concrete diagrams are helpful for children to refer to when "confusions arise with the abstractions" of the algebraic problems with which they are confronted (p. 140). Furthermore, Streefland (1985) has found that "the ratio table is a permanent recording of proportion as an equivalence relation, and in this way contributes to acquiring the correct concept" and "serves the progression in schematising" (p. 91). These researchers have focused on the use of tables to *enhance* or *guide* students' understanding of functions. In contrast, in this chapter we will seek to uncover the understandings about tables, functions, algebra, and mathematics already present in children by analyzing the original self-designed tables constructed by young children. This psychogenetic approach to children's notations is similar to that carried out in the area of literacy by Ferreiro (e.g., Ferreiro, 1988; Ferreiro & Teberosky, 1979) and in the area of musical notations by Bamberger (e.g., 1988).

In our classroom research (see Carraher, Brizuela, & Earnest, 2001; Carraher, Brizuela, & Schliemann, 2000; Carraher, Schliemann, & Brizuela, 2001; Schliemann, Carraher, & Brizuela, 2001), we have noticed that children tend to construct tables that differ significantly from the conventional tables that they are shown by us, their teachers. This has suggested to us that children's re-construction of tables can inform us about how they are working tabular notations into their thinking—their thinking in general and about functions in particular. A case in point is that of a second grader named Joey. When asked to construct a table to display the data we had been working with in a word problem, he began to peek at the printed table on the last page of his handout. As he re-constructed the table, he intermittently flipped to the end page to verify his work and move to the next step. Figure 6.1a shows the table he used as a model, and Figure 6.1b shows his own table. At first glance, he simply transposed the table, organizing the columns by days (even though it was organized by children's names in the original table) and the rows by children. However, he did not place the children's names only once at the beginning of each row. Instead, he wrote the child's initials in each one of the cells. In other words, in Joey's re-construction, Jessica's initial recurs in each cell of row 1, Daniel's initial recurs in each cell of row 2, and Leslie's initial recurs in each cell of row 3.

In this chapter, we explore children's self-designed data tables with the goals of (1) learning about what they consider relevant in the construction of a data table; and (2) learning more about children's understanding of additive functions, as reflected in their self-designed tables.

We will present two sets of connected data. The first set is taken from our work with children in four second-grade classrooms in a public elementary school from a multicultural community, the same one that is described in Chapter 5. Joey, mentioned above, is one of these second graders. These examples are part of our longitudinal work with students as they move from their second through fourth years of schooling. During the second grade, we met with the students once a week during a 6-week period. Our curriculum that semester was centered on an exploration of additive structures. Midway through the semester, we interviewed the children in groups of two or three. The purpose of the interviews was twofold: to learn about the students' understandings of the concepts and to hold more individualized interactions with the students, as learning opportunities. We interviewed a total of 39 children.

The second set of data follows one specific child within that second-grade group: Jennifer. In this set of data, we will follow Jennifer into her third grade, analyzing how her understanding and use of tables change after one year, and how this relates to her understanding of algebraic concepts and relationships as well as of mathematics in general.

	Jessica	Daniel	Leslie
Day 1	7	4	0
Day 2	9	6	2
Day 3	12	9	5
Day 4	14	11	7
Day 7	20		
Day 10		20	
Day 16			20
Any day		X	

(a) The table that Joey used as a model

(b) Joey's table

Figure 6.1. Joey's re-construction of a table.

SECOND GRADE: LOOKING AT CHILDREN'S SELF-DESIGNED TABLES

During the midterm interview we had with the second graders, we presented the students with the problem shown in Figure 6.2 (the same problem that we had presented to Joey, mentioned earlier). After going through the problem, we asked each child to show in a table what had happened in the problem, from Day 1 through Day 3. We did not give the children a model to follow in building their tables, although they had already worked with tables in their classes with us.

The Range of Notations

The children's responses spanned the range from the very idiosyncratic, such as Jennifer's (Figure 6.3), to the more conventional, such as Joseph's (Figure 6.4). Interestingly, Jennifer and Joseph had actually worked to-

---

Day 1:

Jessica, Daniel, and Leslie each has a piggy bank where they keep the money they receive from their grandmother. One day, they counted the money they had and found that Jessica had $7, Daniel had $4, and Leslie had none. They then decided not to spend any more money and keep all the money their grandma would give them in their piggy banks.

Show how much money each one has.

Day 2:

On the second day, Grandma came to visit and gave $2 to each one of the children. They put the money in their piggy banks.

Show what happened.

Day 3:

On the third day, Grandma came to visit and gave $3 to each one of the children.

Show what happened.

How much money does each one have now?

Show in a table what happened from day 1 to day 3.

Figure 6.2. The problem that was presented to the second graders.

Figure 6.3. Jennifer's table.

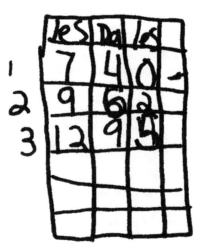

Figure 6.4. Joseph's table.

gether on this problem, even though their responses were radically different. Jennifer explained that she drew a table (literally!), with its four legs. She described the table she had made in the following way:

> See, I wrote days up here (pointing to the word *days*), and then wrote, there was three days, right (pointing to the numbers)? And that is including money (pointing to the dollar bill). And then I drew squares, and it says, . . . on day 2 they got $2 and on day 3 they got $3.

Joseph, however, explained that he did a "regular table . . . it's just got days and names" (maybe feeling slightly intimidated by Jennifer's creation!).

Children's Choice of Variables for Columns and Rows

Of the 39 children interviewed, 22 used time as the variable of their choice for the rows, and the names of the children as headers for the columns. Thus, in most of these children's tables, going down a column also reflects the passing of time. Joseph's table is an example of this kind of construction (see Figure 6.4). In contrast, an example of a table that does not follow this order is that of Joey, in Figure 6.1b.

Explicit and Implicit Information

An analysis of the children's tables also indicates which kind of information they made explicit and which remained implicit. In their tables, children were more likely to make the names of the children in the problem (i.e., Daniel, Jessica, and Leslie) explicit, treating them as information that could not be obliterated from the cells or table. Thus, only 3 of the 39 children (8%) left out the children's names in their tables. An example of a table that left out this information is that of Jessie (Figure 6.5). In Jessie's

Figure 6.5. Jessie's table.

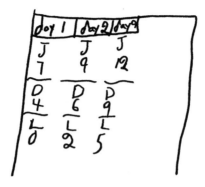

Figure 6.6. Raymond's table.

table, it is hard to discern to whom each of the amounts refer. The fact that there are so few children who obliterated this information may indicate that it is very important for quantities to have some kind of referent or, in this case, "owner" (see Schwartz, 1988, 1996). Along the same lines, 14 of the 39 children (36%) repeat the names of the children in their tables. Raymond's table, for example, seems to indicate that he felt compelled to include the names, by initials, of the children in the problem—the "owners" of each amount—in each one of the cells in his table (Figure 6.6).

In contrast, the second graders we worked with did not always make explicit in their tables the day numbers they were dealing with—that is, the variable of time. Thirteen of the 39 children (33%) did not write the names of the days in their tables (compared with the 3 children who did not write the names of the children). Briana is an example of a child who did not explicitly register the day numbers in her table (Figure 6.7). This

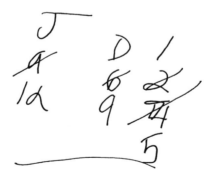

Figure 6.7. Briana's table.

may indicate that in her view, the inclusion of this information did not need to be made explicit.

It seems that the day numbers is information that can be left implicit. Going along the cells (be it down the columns or across the rows, as was done by some children such as Jessie [see Figure 6.5] and Raymond [see Figure 6.6]) shows the passing of time. Some children may think that therefore this information, the variable time, can be left implicit. Additionally, very few children (2 of the 39 children, or 5%) actually repeat the day numbers in their cells (compared with the 13 children who repeated the children's names in their cells). Adam, for example, repeated the information about the day numbers in each one of the cells in his table (Figure 6.8). Moreover, when providing a verbal explanation of his notation during the interview, Adam felt compelled to repeat not only the day numbers but also each character's name, each day:

> Day 1, Jessica had $7. Day 1, Daniel had, uhm, $4, and Day 1 Leslie had zero dollars. Day 2, Jessica had $9. Day 2, Daniel had $6. Day 2, Leslie had $2. Day 3, Jessica had $12. Day 3, uhm, Daniel had $3. Day 3, Leslie had $5.

The choices children make about the kind of information to make explicit and to leave implicit in their tables highlight some of the issues that these children may find relevant in their construction and re-construction of data tables (Ferreiro [1986b] and García-Milà, Teberosky, & Martí [2000] have previously explored this issue of explicit and implicit information). The referents for the amounts are important to them, while an indi-

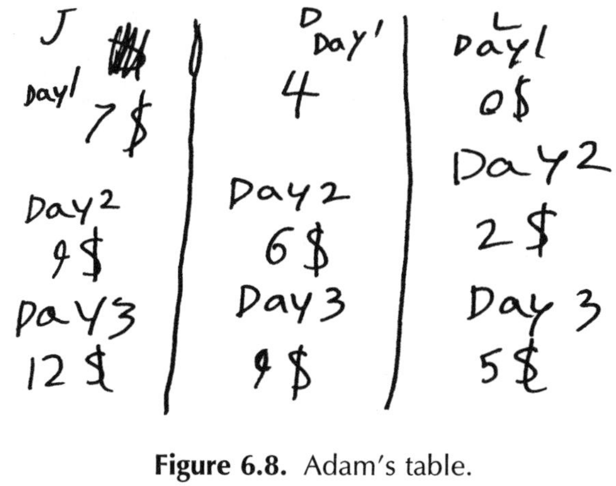

Figure 6.8. Adam's table.

cation of the temporal order of the events is not as important. In children's minds, there may be other ways in which tables can indicate temporal order; the variable of names, however, is one that needs to be made highly explicit.

Looking into Additive Relations

Of the 39 children interviewed, most children (36 of the 39, or 92%) showed in their tables the cumulative amount of money that each child had on each one of the three days—that is, how much money each child *had* and not how much they *got*. Tables such as Joseph's (see Figure 6.4), Briana's (see Figure 6.7), and Adam's (see Figure 6.8) are examples of tables in which only the cumulative amounts are depicted in the tables. However, the other three children showed in their tables the amount of money *gained* each day instead of the total amount of money—that is, how much money they *got* and not how much they *had*. Jennifer's table (see Figure 6.3) is an example of this kind of notation. Another example is the table made by Maria, who shows the amounts gained by drawing a circle around them. The circled parts at the bottom of the notation are the amounts the children *got* from their grandmother on the second and third days (Figure 6.9).

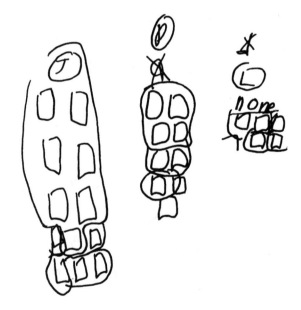

Figure 6.9. Maria's table.

Thus, in thinking about the additive relations they were representing in their tables, most of the children focused on total amounts; that is, on how much each child had on each one of the three days. A variation of this focus can be seen in notations such as Briana's (see Figure 6.7) and Jessie's (see Figure 6.5). In their tables, they crossed out the amount of money the children had on the previous day once they noted how much they had on the following day. Thus, when they moved on to Day 2, they crossed out the amount on Day 1. In their notations, they seem to need to clarify that the amounts represented in each row should not be added to the amounts in the previous rows, but that each new row makes the previous ones invalid. A few children, however, focused on the *differences* between the amounts that the children had on each one of the days, or how much the children *got* on each one of the days. This is the case of Jennifer and Maria described above.

JENNIFER IN THIRD GRADE

During the third grade, we continued to meet with the students once a week during an 8-week period in the fall and an 8-week period in the spring. Our curriculum was then focused on additive structures, variables and unknowns, and equations. Midway through the school year, we interviewed the children individually with the goal of learning how their understanding of additive structures had changed after one year. Jennifer, whose notation of a table during the second grade we discussed earlier (see Figure 6.3), is one of the third graders we interviewed. During the interview, we presented Jennifer and her peers with the problem shown in Figure 6.10. No model table was included at the end of the handout given to the children.

The previous year, in her second grade, Jennifer had drawn a very idiosyncratic table (see Figure 6.3), a "table" complete with its four legs. When she was in third grade, Jennifer reacted very differently to my request to make a table as a way to show the problem we had presented, and she talked about her "table" from the year before.

JENNIFER: I did that bad last year.
BÁRBARA: You did?
JENNIFER: Mh-hm.
BÁRBARA: How do you know?
JENNIFER: 'Cause I drew a table.
BÁRBARA: Ah, you still remember? Yeah? Why do you think that was bad?
JENNIFER: 'Cause I didn't know what it [a table] was.

Mary and John each have a bag with marbles.

- On *Sunday*, they each had the same amount of marbles in their bags.
- On *Monday*, they played marbles with their friends at school, and they each won 5 marbles.
  a. Does Mary have more marbles than John?
  b. Does John have more marbles than Mary?
  c. Do they have the same?
  d. How do you know?

- On *Tuesday*, they played marbles again at school. This time, Mary lost 3 marbles, and John lost 7 marbles.
  a. Does Mary still have the same amount of marbles as John?
  b. How do you know?
  c. What is the difference between the two amounts?

- On *Wednesday*, Mary opened up her bag and found that she had 9 marbles in it.
  d. How many marbles did each of them have on Sunday?
  e. How many marbles did John end up with in his bag on Wednesday?

Show in a table what happened from Sunday to Wednesday.

Figure 6.10. The problem presented to Jennifer
and her peers in third grade.

A year after the first interview reported in this chapter, Jennifer made a more conventional table (Figure 6.11). She used the names of the children as headers for rows, and the days of the week as headers for columns, thus reflecting the passing of time as one moves along the rows. Jennifer's construction was considerably more advanced than her previous table, which did not reflect the passing of time *or* an increase in quantities (of money).

In contrast with her earlier table, where she showed only the days and the amounts earned each day but not the cumulative amounts the children in the problem had, this time Jennifer's table provided a very clear notation of the problem as the amounts of marbles change. As can be seen in Figure 6.11, she now made use of a variable (N) to represent the—unknown—initial amount. After that, she only needed to show how many marbles were gained or lost from that initial amount N. Furthermore, for Tuesday she represented only the total number of marbles gained or lost in one

Figure 6.11. Jennifer's table in third grade.

single step. She was aware that N + 2 represented the total amount of marbles Mary would have on Tuesday if she gained 5 on Monday but then lost 3 on Tuesday.

After Jennifer made her table, I asked her what she thought of her construction, compared to the one she remembered she had made the previous year.

> JENNIFER: It's better.
> BÁRBARA: It's better? Why?
> JENNIFER: 'Cause I didn't mess up. I did, but it's a real math table.

And, exploring what she meant with a "real math table," she explained further.

> JENNIFER: They look like this (pointing to Figure 6.11). The other table I drew last time looked like a table and I made dollars on it. . . . [This table] shows how they did, like uh, like shows how much they have and you could compare them. . . . Like, they both have 7, they both have 12, and then, she has 4 more.
> BÁRBARA: OK. So what do you think that tables are used for in math?
> JENNIFER: To compare . . . You could use them for comparing and you could use them for also to do the math.

Even though no "direct instruction" regarding the conventional way to construct tables had been given to Jennifer and her peers, her approach changed drastically in one year. Granted, she had multiple experiences in which tables were used in different ways during that year. However, from her second to her third grade, Jennifer not only advanced in the way in which she constructed a table. She also developed a meta-understanding of what tables were for. Her final explanation, above, in fact connects to the two uses that Sara gave to her notations for fractions in Chapter 5: to show her solution to a problem (what Jennifer meant by "comparing") but also to help her out in actually solving the problem (Jennifer's "to do the math").

REFLECTIONS

We take seriously the question posed now more than 10 years ago by Kaput (1991) and already presented in Chapter 5: "How do material notations and mental constructions interact to produce new constructions?" (p. 55). While we do not believe that we could answer this question conclusively based on the data presented here, we can indicate that there is a great need to look further and deeper into children's construction of data tables. By developing better understandings both of how their tables evolve and of the understandings about additive relations that are reflected in their notations, we can better serve them as teachers and as curriculum developers. We have begun to unearth some of the understandings that children have about additive relations, as reflected in their notations. Still to be further explored is the interaction of *both* their own constructions and conventional tables with the development of their understandings about additive relations.

Even though their experiences with data tables are few, the second- and third-grade children we worked with have developed sophisticated tabular notations of the data presented in a problem focusing on the progression of money gained over time. They construct data tables that make sense and that reveal the workings of their logic about the problem at hand, and they adequately organize and represent the problem situation. Interestingly, children incorporate into their notations conventional features of data tables. More than half the children we interviewed chose for the columns and rows the variables of time and names. Additionally, information such as showing the children's names seems to be relevant to students when they construct these tables, which is consistent with Schwartz's (1988, 1996) suggestion regarding the importance of having referents for quantities. Furthermore, data tables seem to help uncover children's conceptions and understandings about additive relations.

Jennifer, Nathan, and Jeffrey: Relationships Among Different Mathematical Notations

BÁRBARA: But what do you think [the crossing of the lines] means? Look at the lines. Why are they crossing there? . . . Where do they cross?

NATHAN: At . . . fourteen and seven. Fourteen and seven.

BÁRBARA (correcting): At seven, fourteen.

JENNIFER: (Looking at her piece of paper and pointing to her vector and number line notations) That's what I said [before]!

This chapter focuses on the interactions between different kinds of notations and the kinds of understandings that children can develop as a result of notating problems in multiple ways. Recently, the NCTM (2000) has acknowledged the importance of "translating" or establishing relationships between multiple notations:

> Different representations often illuminate different aspects of a complex concept or relationship. . . . Thus, in order to become deeply knowledgeable about [a specific mathematical concept]—and many other concepts in school mathematics—students will need a variety of representations that support their understanding. (p. 68)

Jeanne Bamberger's (1990) work in the area of musical notations also encourages the use of multiple notations through the confronting of "differences and similarities that [emerge] as [the students move] across materials, sensory modalities, and kinds of descriptions" (p. 39). Specifically, in this chapter I will focus on the *"generative value,"* as Bamberger describes it, of establishing relationships between different kinds of mathematical notations. As Bamberger (1990) puts it, establishing these relationships contains an immanent potential and could result in critical transformations in children's sense-making of symbolic expressions. She has both described the relationships one person might establish among different "symbolic expressions" and discussed the active confrontation of notations made by different people. This latter confrontation process, she explains, can help us become increasingly aware not just of what we have noticed, but also of what we have not noticed that others have found meaningful (Bamberger & Ziporyn, 1992).

In the area of mathematics education, Judah Schwartz has also focused on the importance of offering students multiple possibilities and ways to represent understandings. Schwartz places much importance on students being able to use different kinds of notations—such as symbolic language, numerical language, graphical language, and natural language—with some agility (Schwartz & Yerushalmy, 1995).

Also in the area of mathematics education, Goldin has recently highlighted the importance of what he calls building "relationships among representations":

> Effective mathematics thinking involves understanding the relationships among different representations of "the same" concept as well as the structural similarities (and differences) among representational systems. That is, the student must develop adequate internal representations for interacting with various systems. (Goldin & Shteingold, 2001, p. 9)

Given past research and literature, at least three questions come up regarding the relationships between multiple notations:

1. What is gained when children can establish relationships among different kinds of notations?
2. What is the impact of establishing these kinds of relationships?
3. How does one child's notation relate to the notations proposed by others?

In order to begin to address these questions, let us now turn to the example that will be the focus of this chapter, that of Jennifer, Nathan, and Jeffrey working on the "Best Deal" problem.

DETAILS OF THE STUDY

The data I will report in this chapter comes from the work with third graders described in Chapter 6. I will concentrate on a particular interview carried out with three third graders, at the end of the school year, in June. We had been working with these children since the middle of their second grade. We had chosen to carry out group interviews at the end of their academic year as a way to document and assess their progress and difficulties and the effect of our work in the classroom. We chose a mix of students for each group interviewed and also consulted with their classroom teacher regarding the composition of the interview groups. In each group, we were striving for a diversity of ways of thinking as well as performance levels in mathematics. The interviews had both a research and a teaching component, and as I carried out this particular interview, I was both researcher and teacher. I was interested in investigating the children's thinking about the problem; throughout the interview, however, I also gave the students some guidance and suggestions, wanting to lead them in a particular direction while at the same time wanting to investigate what the children would do with my particular suggestions (see Duckworth, 1996, for a thoughtful narrative about the intersection between research and teaching).

Jennifer, Nathan, and Jeffrey were peers in the same third-grade classroom, but had not been in the same second-grade classroom. I was their mathematics teacher during our once-a-week, 16-week intervention. I also carried out this particular interview with the children. Jennifer, whom we discussed in Chapter 6, was a very active and vocal participant in mathematics classes. Her parents were originally from Brazil. Although her answers to problems and questions were not always correct, she had a way of verbalizing her thought processes and of representing problems that was very helpful in discussions in the whole group. Nathan, one of the few Anglo children in his class, was also a very active member. Most often, his answers were not on target, and he struggled with some of the mathematical content that we presented in class. Of the three, Jeffrey was the most quiet student. Of Latino origin, he would usually only participate if he was sure of his response. His interventions were usually correct, but in general, his teachers' perceptions of him were that he was not very smart and did not do very well in school.

THE PROBLEM PRESENTED TO THE CHILDREN

Figure 7.1 shows the problem presented to the children. It was different from problems presented in class up to that time given the fact that they had to consider two functions simultaneously. Previously, we had only asked them to consider one linear function at a time, and we had never asked them to compare them. In terms of the notations to which they had been exposed and become accustomed in their classes with us, they had

---

Let's Make a Deal!

Raymond has some money.

His grandmother offers him two deals:

    Deal 1: She will double his money.

    Deal 2: She will triple his money and then take away $7.

Raymond wants to choose the best deal. What should he do?

How would you figure out and *show him* what is best to do?

Is one deal *always* better? Show on this piece of paper.

Figure 7.1. The problem presented to Jennifer, Nathan, and Jeffrey.

used number lines, vectors, Cartesian coordinate graphs, and function tables on a regular basis.

THE CHILDREN'S REACTIONS TO THE PROBLEM

Right away, Jennifer and Nathan said they preferred the first deal because it involved *doubling* money. They were concerned with the second deal because the grandmother would *take away* $7. They explained to me that they would not like to be in a situation where money was *taken away* from them. Jeffrey agreed that Raymond should choose Deal 1. Right after this, however, Jennifer said, "First we have to find out how much money he has." Thus, she was acknowledging that she felt uncomfortable, to some degree, with the fact that we were dealing with an unknown amount. This happened even though we had been working with unknown and variable amounts in different kinds of problems since their second grade. After asking how we could find out how much money Raymond had, and a short discussion among the three students, Nathan finally said that we couldn't figure out how much money he started out with:

> NATHAN: Because [the problem] doesn't even say. "She'll double the money . . . " (Paraphrasing the wording in the problem.)
> JENNIFER: It just says he has some money.
> NATHAN: *Some* money.

Then, I proposed that they try the problem out first with $4 ("Let's say he has $4") and then that they try it out with $5 ("Well, let's say he has 5, OK?"). The children worked with tokens, using them to represent how much money Raymond started and ended with. In both cases, the children found that Deal 1 was better. Jennifer said, "If you have more money, and you go with Deal 1, the more money you will have." I proposed that we try to figure out if Deal 2 was *ever* better than Deal 1. Nathan proposed to try out the case in which Raymond started out with $8. When they tried out this case, they found that Deal 2 was better. In this way, after 10 minutes had gone by in the interview, the children had figured out that sometimes Deal 1 was better, and other times Deal 2 was better. Finally, the children tried out what would happen if Raymond started out with $7. They figured out that when Raymond started out with $7, both deals were equal. At this point, I came back to the original question posed in the problem about what Raymond should do—which deal he should choose—and the following conversation developed, at 15 minutes into the interview:

JEFFREY: Maybe Deal 2. Deal 2, because it worked out with 8.

BÁRBARA: Worked out with eight. But what happens with seven?

NATHAN: It equals.

JEFFREY: At seven it equals.

BÁRBARA: So again, I'm going to ask you the question. What should he do?

JENNIFER: Deal number 2.

NATHAN: Number 2.

BÁRBARA: Always?

JENNIFER: No.

BÁRBARA: When?

JENNIFER: Like, first if the grandma's going to ask you those questions, if you want deal number one or number two, you should try it out first, which one's better.

NATHAN: Depending on how much money he has.

BÁRBARA: Oooh, did you hear Nathan? Depending on how much money he has. So, how, like what would you say to your grandma? If you were Raymond, what would you say?

NATHAN: If I had $7, I'd do deal number 1 because I'd double it to 14. Not [deal] number 2, because you'll just take $7 away. (This statement by Nathan reveals that he is still uncomfortable with having money *taken away* from him. Given a choice, even though he has already acknowledged that for $7, Deals 1 and 2

are equal, he still prefers Deal 1, so that money isn't taken away
from him).

BÁRBARA: But if you have seven then it doesn't make a difference,
does it?

JENNIFER: Nope.

. . .

BÁRBARA: So you said that . . .

JENNIFER: Like if you have $7 you can pick either one.

BÁRBARA: And, and what if you had less than $7?

NATHAN: Then you have to go with [deal] number 1.

JENNIFER: Number 1.

BÁRBARA: And when do you pick [deal] number 2?

NATHAN: If you have like fourteen.

JEFFREY: Eight.

. . .

BÁRBARA: If you have eight. So if you have like . . .

JENNIFER: So if you have seven it's equal, it's right in the middle (gesturing a midpoint with her hands). And if you have higher than
seven you go with number 2 (gesturing with her hands toward
the right of the midpoint she has designated), and lower than
seven then deal number 1 (gesturing with her hands toward the
left of the original midpoint).

This first gesture presented by Jennifer begins our discussion regarding
relationships among different kinds of notations. Jennifer's gesture mir-
rored almost exactly the formation of a number line. It is interesting to
note that number lines had been used quite extensively by our research
team in her third-grade classroom. Initially, we had introduced them as a
way of extending the students' "internal" or mental number lines that finished off abruptly at zero and did not extend beyond that into negative
numbers. We also began to use number lines in her class as a tool for
performing computations. In addition, we introduced the use of what we
came to call a "variable" number line, in which the zero point was replaced
by N, a variable quantity, and the positions varied to the right of N from
$N + 1$ to $N + 2$, $N + 3$, and so on. To the left of N, the positions varied
from $N - 1$ to $N - 2$, $N - 3$, and so on. In her third-grade classroom, Jennifer was recognized as the most avid user of number lines. Even when we
as instructors and researchers had assumed the number line topic to have
been "covered," Jennifer was able to consistently and effectively use the
number line as a tool for notating and solving problems that were presented to her, including problems relating to heights that we thought would
be difficult for children to notate in a horizontal as opposed to a vertical

fashion. Jennifer had thus internalized what had been originally an external and conventional notation, introduced by her teacher, to such an extent that it became a mathematical tool for her. Jennifer's gesture revealed, once more, the extent to which she had incorporated this type of notation into her understanding about mathematics.

Jennifer's gesture involved a first important relationship: between a conceptual understanding about the problem and a body gesture. In fact, recent research has shown ways in which gestures *embody* and represent conceptual understandings (see Roth, 2001, for a recent review of research on gestures). Jennifer is representing, through her body, her understanding of the problem.

After Jennifer provided the group with this summary of her understanding of the problem, I asked the children if there was a way to show, on their pieces of paper, which was the better deal. Jennifer's initial *relationship* had been between her conceptual understanding and her use of oral language and then a body gesture. Now, I was asking them for a new kind of relationship: between their conceptual understanding and an external paper-and-pencil notation. Oral language, however, remained a possible intermediate step for the children to use. However, forcing them to use external pencil-and-paper notations was a didactic maneuver that highlights, once again, the fuzzy distinctions between research and teaching (see Duckworth, 1996).

THE CHILDREN'S NOTATIONS

Jennifer was the first one to attempt a notation for the problem. Figure 7.2 shows her initial number line and vector notations. Jennifer seemed to mirror her initial bodily gesture in her vector notation: She marked 7 as the middle point and then focused on what happened before and after 7. In both the vector and the number line notations, she marked that 7 was "right in the middle," further emphasizing in the number line notation that 7 was where both deals were equal by writing an equal sign above the 7. She also used natural language (see upper-right corner) to express a similar understanding of the problem: "Deal 1 when under 7 deal 2 over 7 When 7 either one." As mentioned, both vector and number line notations had been presented in her classroom beforehand. However, the instructions presented to Jennifer in this problem did not give her any indication about the use of these particular notations. We might assume, therefore, that both vectors and number lines had become part of her expressive repertoire to such an extent that she was able to use them spontaneously to notate her conceptual understandings. This highlights the complexity inherent in the

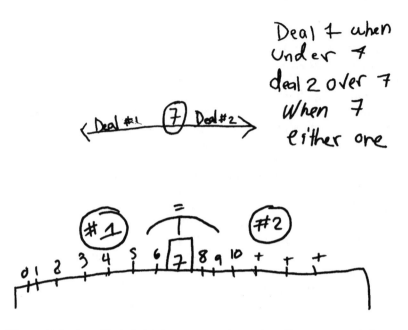

Figure 7.2. Jennifer's initial vector and number line representations.

relationships established between different notations: An initial conventional notation had been assimilated to such an extent by Jennifer that it was transformed into an internal or mental representation. This process in Jennifer seems to reflect Goldin's position regarding what he calls a representational perspective, contrasting with behaviorist and constructivist approaches. This representational perspective

> involves explicit focus on both the external and the internal, with the utmost attention given to the interplay between them. Through interaction with structured external representations in the learning environment, students' internal representation systems develop. The students can then generate new external representations. (Goldin & Shteingold, 2001, p. 8)

Nathan and Jeffrey followed Jennifer's suit. Nathan also adopted the vector and number line notations (see Figure 7.3). In a sense, we might say that he "copied" from Jennifer. As previously shown (see Joey's case in Chapter 6, for example; see also Ferreiro & Teberosky, 1979, for a similar analysis in the area of written language), however, copying is not a mere transcription but shows similar kinds of transformations as those in-

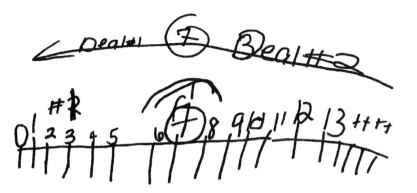

Figure 7.3. Nathan's initial vector and number line representations.

volved in transforming speech into written language, for example (see Olson, 1994).

Nathan did not include an equal sign, and he did not write out the numbers on the number line beyond 13; he just wrote a series of plus signs. We might wonder or hypothesize whether Nathan and Jeffrey also had to establish relationships between Jennifer's bodily gesture and her notation and finally with their own notation. Or did they make relationships between their conceptual understandings and their notations? (The similarities between their notations and Jennifer's make it more likely that Jennifer's notations mediated between their conceptual understandings and their first notations.) Or did they establish relationships between Jennifer's oral explanation or their own oral explanations and, finally, their notations?

Jeffrey followed suit with a notation that in spite of borrowing from Jennifer's idea was even more schematic—it displayed only the essential pieces of information to allow one to make sense of the connections between the problem and the notation (Figure 7.4). Again, he also showed before 7 and after 7.

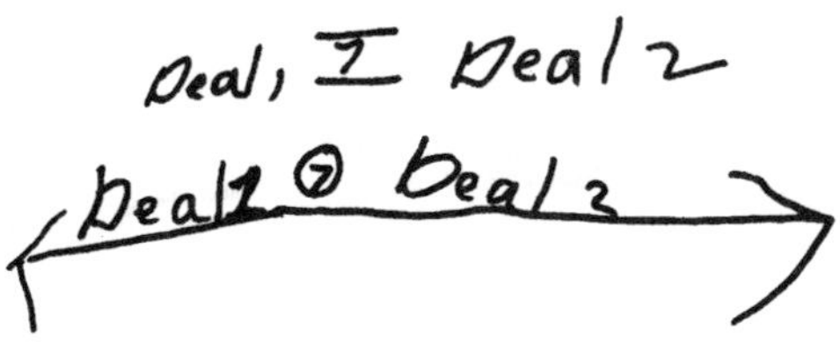

Figure 7.4. Jeffrey's initial vector representation.

These initial notations, through number lines and vectors, were, as mentioned earlier, the initial relationships that Jennifer, Nathan, and Jeffrey established between conceptual understandings and notations. They represented in an almost mirror fashion the understandings and explanations the children had verbalized earlier in the interview, assuming that the verbal explanations were another way of representing that conceptual understanding. Wanting to push them further, and after verifying that the children could not spontaneously think of other ways of notating the problem, I proposed that they build tables and graphs (understood among us as Cartesian coordinate graphs) to show what was happening in the problem. The children had used function tables and graphs during their lessons with us. In fact, they had both made their own graphs and worked on interpreting graphs and tables that we presented them with in our lessons. As soon as I made this suggestion, each of the children picked up their pencils and started working. Jennifer chose to do a graph, and Nathan and Jeffrey chose to focus on tables. Here I will not elaborate on the relationships that might exist between conceptual understandings and notations. Instead, I will describe first their notations and then the relationships among different notations.

Figure 7.5 shows Jennifer's initial organization of the Cartesian graph. Jennifer began confidently plotting out the two axes and numbering each

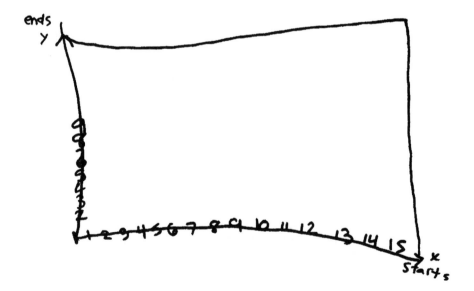

Figure 7.5. Jennifer's initial organization of the Cartesian graph.

one. Then, she faced the dilemma of deciding what variables to choose for each axis. When she suggested using Deal 1 for the x axis and Deal 2 for the y axis, I suggested that instead she could use Raymond's starting amount of money for the x axis and Raymond's ending amount of money for the y axis. This was a pedagogical decision I made at the time, given that I was interested in fostering a conversation about the connections and similarities/differences between the information presented in the tables and that presented in the graph. I did not think that Jennifer's proposal for setting up the graph would lead to this intended discussion.

Finally Jennifer moved on to large butcher-block paper to show the two linear functions on the Cartesian graph. Again, I hoped that the use of large butcher-block paper would facilitate the kind of discussion that I was striving for during the interview. This was another pedagogical decision I made, highlighting once again the connections between interviewing research and teaching (see Duckworth, 1996).

Jeffrey and Nathan worked on their tables side by side, occasionally consulting but mostly stating that they were each "doing their own thing." Jeffrey's table (see Figure 7.6) was built in a conventional fashion, with the first column showing the amount of money Raymond would start with, and the second and third columns the amount of money he would end up with if he chose Deal 1 or Deal 2, respectively. In his table, it was interesting to note how Jeffrey added descriptions of what he did to get the answers he needed in each column (i.e., "counts by 2's," "counts by 3's").

Nathan's table, built at the same time as Jeffrey's, was organized in a very different way (see Figure 7.7). First, Nathan's table was less conventional than Jeffrey's. In each row, Nathan tried out a different amount of money, without the systematic exhaustion of the different amounts of money that Jeffrey went through in his table, as he went down row by row. Second, Nathan needed to make *explicit* in his table information that Jeffrey assumed to be *implicit* (see Chapter 6 for a presentation on implicit and explicit information): While Nathan added a third column to clarify which would be the better deal for that amount of money, this information remained implicit in Jeffrey's table, where you could compare each row and the results obtained in columns 2 and 3 to gather the same information.

THE CHILDREN'S INTERPRETATIONS
OF JENNIFER'S GRAPH

Once the three children were finished with their notations, I asked them to come together and initially try to interpret the graph constructed by Jenni-

Figure 7.6. Jeffrey's table.

fer. In this process, three moments merit highlighting in terms of the relationships that were developed. In the first, Jennifer found a connection between her graph and her initial vector and number line notations. In the second, Jeffrey spontaneously and methodically used his table to interpret the graph. Finally, in the third moment, the three children tried to figure out the similarities and differences between the story told in the table and that told in the graph.

Jennifer's Realization About the Crossing of the Lines in Her Vector Notation

The initial focus point in our conversation concerned what each line in the graph was representing—that is, which was Deal 1 and which was Deal

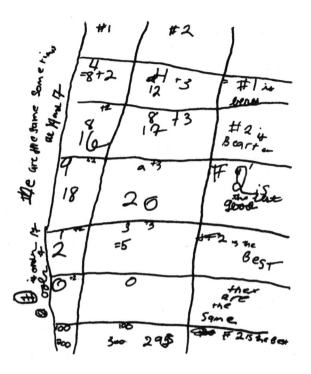

Figure 7.7. Nathan's table.

2. Once this was clarified—fairly quickly—the discussion turned to what the crossing of the lines could mean. This was the conversation that took place:

> BÁRBARA: But what do you think [the crossing of the lines] means? Look at the lines. Why are they crossing there? Where do they cross?
>
> NATHAN: At . . . fourteen and seven. Fourteen and seven.
>
> BÁRBARA: (Correcting) At seven, fourteen.
>
> JENNIFER: (Looking at her piece of paper and pointing to her vector and number line notations) That's what I said [before]!
>
> BÁRBARA: (Addressing Jennifer) Why do you think they cross at that point, and not at any other point? Why do you . . . Why do you think? Jennifer, do you have any idea? Why do you think that the two lines cross at seven, and not at eight, or at nine, or at ten? Why?

JENNIFER: (Grabbing a marker and making an equal sign on the graph exactly above the point where the two lines cross) They equal. When you do the Deal 1 and Deal 2, they're equal to each other.

Although Jennifer had not initially realized that she had already answered, in a different way, through her number line and vector notations, the question I was asking ("Why do the two lines cross at seven?"), once she was able to realize that 7 was the cutoff number on her vector and number line notations and also the crossing point in the graph, she was able to see the connection between the two notations: "That's what I said!" We could also hypothesize that she added a third notation by adding the equal sign above the crossing point in her graph. Given the fact that she only verbalized her understanding and added this equal sign *after* she realized the connection between the graph and her initial notations, we could also hypothesize that the relationships established among the different notations— graph, vector, and number line—helped her to make this connection. Additionally, she only expressed her understanding regarding the crossing of the lines *after* this relationship was established—thus we could further hypothesize that the relationships aided in her understanding of the graphical notation itself. That is, as Bamberger (1990) would say, the development of the relationship had a "generative value" by facilitating her understanding of the Cartesian coordinate graph. Regarding the kind of impact that the establishment of these relationships had for Jennifer, her understanding of each of the notation systems—number line, vector, and Cartesian graph— was made slightly more complex by the realization of the connections and similarities that existed among them. Furthermore, her understanding of the problem itself and of Raymond's dilemma was further developed by these relationships among the notations.

Jeffrey's Use of His Table to Understand the Graph

The first connection Jeffrey made between his table and the graph concerned the crossing of the lines. When Jennifer provided the preceding explanation for the crossing of the lines, I observed that Jeffrey was looking very intently at his table (see Figure 7.6). I asked Jeffrey a question:

BÁRBARA: Did you hear that, Jeffrey? Jennifer thinks they cross at seven because seven is where the deals are equal. Does that sound good? (Jeffrey keeps checking his table) Did you get the

same answer on your table? (Jeffrey nods and points to the seventh row in his table)

JEFFREY: Fourteen, fourteen.

BÁRBARA: Fourteen, fourteen.

In a sense, it seemed that Jeffrey was using his table to *corroborate* Jennifer's assessment. The lines in Jennifer's graph crossed at 7 and 14 and his
table had a row showing 7-14-14.

The second connection Jeffrey made between the table and the graph
concerned the patterns of the lines before and after the crossing point. This
time, Jeffrey used his table not to *corroborate* the information that he was
gathering from the graph and Jennifer was summarizing, but as a *tool to
understand* what was actually happening in the graph:

BÁRBARA: And look at the graph. What's going on? What's going
on, look at what's going on before seven and after seven. Do
you see what's going on, Jeffrey?

JEFFREY: (Looking intently at his table and looking up to the graph;
continually looking up and down between his table and the
graph)

BÁRBARA: What are you trying to figure out? What are you trying to
figure out?

JEFFREY: Whoa!! (Emphatically and excited) After this half (making
a sweeping movement above the intersection of 7 and 14), the
deal number 2 is greater. And here the deal number 2 [*sic*] is better (making a sweeping movement below the intersection of 7
and 14).

BÁRBARA: Deal number one you mean.

JEFFREY: Deal number one.

BÁRBARA: So, Jeff, so why? So you're saying that here deal number
one is better (changing what Jeffrey was saying, I make a sweeping movement to the left of the intersection of 7 and 14), and
here deal number two is better (making a sweeping movement to
the right of the intersection of 7 and 14). Is that what you're saying? (Then drawing a vertical line—dividing left and right parts
of the graph, or before 7 and after 7 on the *x* axis—that goes
through the intersection point at 7 and 14.)

JEFFREY: Yup. After this line (insisting on a horizontal line that goes
through the intersection point and that divides the graph into
above and below or before and after 14 on the *y* axis).

BÁRBARA: Which line? (Jeffrey gestures a horizontal line through 7 and 14.) Oh, should I draw one [line] there too? Do you (addressing Jennifer) want to draw it? (Jennifer draws a horizontal line that goes through the intersection of 7 and 14, focusing on Jeffrey's interpretation of the graph.)

After looking intently at his table and consulting back and forth between his table and the graph, Jeffrey was able to provide an interpretation for the graph that we assume he would not have been able to provide had he not had his table (hence his expression of "Whoa!" after finding a connection between his table and the graph). First his table was a *corroboration*, and then it was a *tool to understand* the graph. In both cases, relationships between one and the other aided in the understanding of a notation, as well as of Raymond's dilemma presented in the problem itself.

Similarities and Differences Between the Stories Told in the Table and in the Graph

Finally, I myself suggested seeking similarities and differences between the graph Jennifer built and the tables that Nathan and Jeffrey built, focusing specifically at this point on Jeffrey's table, given that this was the children's natural inclination:

BÁRBARA: So does, Jeffrey, does your table . . . let Nathan and Jennifer look at your table. Nathan and Jennifer, if you look at Jeffrey's table, can you figure out where the deals are equal? Look at his table. Look at his table, can you figure out where deal number one and deal number two are equal?

NATHAN: This one right here (pointing to the seventh row on Jeffrey's table).

BÁRBARA: Where are they equal?

NATHAN: Seven.

BÁRBARA: How can you tell they're equal?

JENNIFER: This is the same thing (pointing to the seventh row on Jeffrey's table and to the intersection point in the graph). This [the table] is the answer sheet to this [the graph].

BÁRBARA: Can you tell us why? Actually, can you look at [Jeffrey's] table, Jennifer, and tell us? Remember how you were using this graph to figure out which was a better deal and when? Can you use the table to figure out the same thing? Jeffrey, and Nathan, can you look at Jeffrey's table and do the same thing you did with Jennifer's graph? Look at the table.

A conversation then developed about which line was Deal 1 and which was Deal 2 on the graph:

BÁRBARA: Where [on the graph] is the deal equal?
JENNIFER: Seven.
BÁRBARA: How do you know?
JENNIFER: Fourteen, fourteen.
BÁRBARA: So fourteen, fourteen, so there it's equal. When is deal number one better? Look at the table and not at the graph. When is it better?
JEFFREY: On the less numbers.
BÁRBARA: Less than what?
JEFFREY: Less than the big numbers.
BÁRBARA: (Clarifying) Less than seven. Less than seven deal number one is better. Do you think that that's being shown in this table?
JENNIFER: Yes.
BÁRBARA: How? Look at the table. How can you tell that when it's less than seven deal number one is better? How can you tell?
JENNIFER: Because the numbers are bigger?
BÁRBARA: For what deal?
ALL: Deal number one.
JEFFREY: Deal number one only works for the less numbers, and number two works for the big numbers up here [*sic*] (pointing to the bottom part of the table, to numbers beyond 7).
BÁRBARA: After . . . ?
ALL: After seven.

Jennifer explained that Jeffrey's table was the "answer sheet" for figuring out what was going on in the graph she built. In this way, she was expressing how the table was helping her to understand the graph (even though she was the creator of the graph!). Once again, as in Jeffrey's case in the previous section, we find that establishing relationships between notations can be a *tool for understanding* a particular notation. For Jennifer, having been able to earlier figure out what was going on in the graph didn't automatically mean that she was able to figure out what was going on in the table. The same is true of the reverse situation: Her having figured out what was going on in the table became an opportunity to re-interpret the graph she had already interpreted earlier. It is worthwhile to note that the children spontaneously chose the table that Jeffrey constructed as opposed to Nathan's when they moved between tables and graph. A possible explanation for this is the fact that the organization of Jeffrey's data and table made it easier to compare across graph and table. Once again, the impact of the establishment of the relationships between notations can be seen in the depth of the understandings that children were able to develop regarding both the problem and the notation systems.

REFLECTIONS

As mentioned earlier, both in the work of Bamberger (1990) and Goldin (Goldin & Shteingold, 2001), the importance of establishing relationships between notations is highlighted. These relationships have "generative value" (Bamberger, 1990) of different sorts. For example, as we saw in the interview presented in this chapter, the relationships permit students, such as Jeffrey, to *corroborate* an understanding about the problem that they had developed as a result of interacting with one of the notations and with an explanation provided by a peer. In Jeffrey's case, his looking at the graph corroborated for him that 7 was a cutoff point that he had originally observed in his table. In addition, the relationships became a tool for understanding different notations. In fact, initial interpretations that were developed in isolation of any relationship seemed to be transformed as a result of the relationships established between the different notations. This was illustrated by Jennifer and Jeffrey. We can argue that the initial challenge faced by Jennifer, Nathan, and Jeffrey was that of establishing relationships between their developing conceptual understandings about the problem—arrived at through reflection and the manipulation of objects—and a symbolic notation of that understanding on paper. As we have learned from David Olson (1994) regarding the relationships between oral and written language, this relationship is anything but automatic. In fact, it involves complex and deep transformations of the initial understandings, thus demystifying the idea that establishing these relationships is a simple mirroring process.

Although at this point we can only speculate about the potential impact that the relationships had on Jennifer, Nathan, and Jeffrey's *conceptual* understanding about linear functions, we can speak about the impact the relationship had on their understanding of the different notations as well as of the "Best Deal" problem. Furthermore, their interview provides an illumination and illustration of the kinds of suggestions being put forth by NCTM (2000):

> Different representations often illuminate different aspects of a complex concept or relationship. . . . Thus, in order to become deeply knowledgeable about [a specific mathematical concept]—and many other concepts in school mathematics—students will need a variety of representations that support their understanding. (p. 68)

Final Reflections

Do notations merely express what people understand or do they also influence thought and reasoning themselves? According to Cobb (2000), symbol usage is fundamental to how people can understand and use mathematical concepts. Symbolizing is integral to mathematical activity. Furthermore, the relationship between notations and concepts is interactive: Understanding the connections between them can enrich both the notations and the concepts themselves. As Cobb (2000) explains, "The way that symbols are used and the meanings they come to have are mutually constitutive and emerge together" (p. 18). As Lerner and Sadovsky (1994) have shown in their work, the learning of concepts and of notations occurs simultaneously. However, there is still a pervasive assumption within elementary mathematics education that representational skills are secondary to conceptual understanding. In this position, the rich interaction between understanding and notations is lost. As Nunes and Bryant (1996) lament:

> Much more attention has been given to the logic of mathematics than to conventional mathematical systems by people doing research on mathematical development. The relative neglect of conventional systems is a pity because what little we do know suggests that they play an important part in children's mathematical thinking. In particular, there is a rather subtle relationship between children's logical development and their knowledge of these conventional systems. This relationship is so important that it is actually impossible for us to understand the connection between logical and mathematical development without also knowing about children's acquaintance with conventional mathematical systems. (p. 244)

Through a focus on the interaction and connections between both, students' mathematical development can be supported and enriched. Nunes and Bryant's (1996) position is close to that put forth by Cobb (2000):

> The assumed reflexive relationship between symbol use and mathematical meaning implies that a student's use of symbols involves some type of mean-

ing, and that the development of meaning involves modifications in ways of symbolizing. Viewed in these terms, teaching and instructional design both involve attempts to support the development of students' ways of symbolizing as part of the process of supporting the development of mathematical meaning. (p. 19)

This reflexive relationship and, moreover, a vision for mathematical notations as being *constructed* by learners is not something that has always been accepted. For example, in a 1993 paper, Ball describes her experience with teaching a third-grade mathematics class a unit on negative numbers. Toward the end of her paper, she writes:

> Certainly mathematical conventions are not matters for discovery and reinvention—for instance, how we record numbers or what a square is. But that 6 + (−6) must equal zero, or that an even number plus an odd number will always be odd, or that the probability of rolling a seven with a standard dice is 6/36 are things that children can—through conjecture, explanation, and discussion—create. (p. 393)

Kamii, who like Ball has argued in other venues that children construct and create mathematical ideas, considers that some knowledge can be constructed, while other knowledge should be transmitted, or delivered through "instruction":

> Young children literally reinvent arithmetic. . . . [Piaget] argued that logico-mathematical knowledge is invented by each child, that is, it is constructed by each child from within. It cannot be discovered or learned by transmission from the environment, except for the conventional mathematical signs (such as "=") and the notational system, which constitute the most superficial part of arithmetic. (1985, p. xii)

Elsewhere, she has also explained that "upon hearing the preceding statements, some people conclude that I want children to reinvent everything in mathematics, including algebra. I think the role of instruction must increase as children grow older" (1989, p. 14). This illustrates what I consider to be an artificial separation between knowledge that *can* and that *cannot* be constructed. Kamii has recently revised this position in her second edition of *Young Children Reinvent Arithmetic* (2000). Specifically, she has added a chapter on representations, in which she addresses the kinds of representations that children make for incipient number concepts. She focuses on their spontaneously developed representations. In addition, she has not included in the new edition her harsher criticisms of a focus on representations as being "constructed."

In this book, we have seen numerous examples of children *constructing* mathematical notations of different kinds: the written number system (including symbols within the system, such as punctuation marks, which go beyond just numbers as elements of the system) in George (Chapter 2), Paula (Chapter 3), and Thomas (Chapter 4); fractions in Sara (Chapter 5); data tables, Cartesian coordinate graphs, vectors, number lines, and natural language in Jennifer, Nathan, Jeffrey, and their peers (Chapters 6 and 7). Further, the examples show that there is a *constructive process* involved in children's learning of complex notations, such as data tables and graphs, as well as seemingly inconsequential symbols, such as commas and periods. We have also seen the ways in which notations and conceptual understandings interact. Cases in point are Sara's use of her notations to help her think about the conceptual issues behind problems dealing with fractions (see Chapter 5), and Jennifer, Nathan, and Jeffrey's approach to the "Best Deal" problem and the way in which they used data tables and graphs to further understand a problem dealing with two functions (see Chapter 7). All these children are using the notations they develop as tools for understanding and solving problems.

The construction of notations cannot happen separately from the construction of conceptual aspects in mathematics. These aspects go hand in hand. Notations play an important role in the acquisition of numerical concepts (Lerner & Sadovsky, 1994). However, when previous research has separated these aspects, it has tended either to ignore the written aspects by giving the conceptual aspects a main protagonist role or to reduce the learning of notations to a perceptive-motor exercise. We have seen that learning mathematical notations entails far more than developing perceptive-motor skills.

Moreover, the data presented in this book illustrate the rich and important interaction between children's invented notations and the conventional notations they are taught and are surrounded by. As diSessa and his colleagues explain, the interaction between the spontaneous and conventional representations is important: "Spontaneous representations used by children . . . set a meaningful context in which 'proper' [representations] could be introduced" (diSessa et al., 1991, p. 122). By focusing on the interaction and connections between both, students' mathematical development can be supported and enriched.

The two main points explored throughout this book—that there is a constant interaction between mathematical notations and conceptual understandings and that there is a similar interplay between invented and conventional mathematical notations—pervade each of the other issues put forth. Similarly, connections established with the history of mathematical notations pervade each one of the chapters—the similarities between the events in the history of mathematical notations and children's development of mathematical notations highlight the types of difficulties encountered by both mathematicians of antiquity and contemporary children. The children presented in Chapters 2, 3, and 4—George, Paula, and Thomas—are seen in their early learning about mathematical notations putting together rules for how the number system works. They are seen developing not only understandings about the elements that are part of the system but also understandings about relationships between elements. The important ideas these children and those in other chapters develop underscore the need to think about mathematical notations as an integral part of mathematical understandings and concepts, as well as far more than fine-motor type skills.

The data presented throughout this book also illustrate the importance of Piaget's theory as a framework, as discussed in Chapter 1. Piaget's considerations and descriptions of the learning process provide a relevant lens for analyzing how children learn about mathematical notations. Piaget conceived of learning as a dialectical process composed of assimilation and accommodation. Assimilation is the process through which we transform the external world to make it an integral part of ourselves. Accommodation is the creative moment in learning, as we transform our cognitive structures in order to assimilate new experiences. Piaget (1936/1969, 1936/1977) explained that accommodation starts as an early differentiation of schemes and then becomes an active search for novelty.

Piaget's conception of the learning process pertains to specific cases of children learning mathematical notations because children are constantly assimilating various aspects of conventional mathematical notations that they can grasp. At the same time, they transform or accommodate the ideas that they develop about mathematical notations as a result of this constant and interactive assimilation and accommodation (Piaget, 1936/1969, 1936/1977). Children of a very young age already have ideas about written numbers and how they work and about other mathematical notations. From birth they begin to interact with numbers. By the time they enter school, the constant assimilation of data and accommodation of their cognitive structures leads children to have already developed very complex and interesting ideas.

In addition to assimilation and accommodation, Piaget's research about equilibration and dis-equilibrium is relevant in analyzing children's learning of mathematical notations. Piaget believed that a loss of equilibrium, or dis-equilibrium, could lead to the construction of new actions (i.e., a re-equilibration), as a way to a new equilibrium that would grant the learner greater stability than the previous equilibrium, through the introduction into the subject's field of new elements and relations. Dis-equilibriums could thus lead to transformations through inventions that modified and enriched the subject's previous schemes. In other words, Piaget conceived of thought as naturally dialectical, as an ongoing succession of dis-equilibrium and re-equilibration.

Related to the process of assimilation and accommodation, the new situation or information that the child encounters may not have brought about a sense of dis-equilibrium in the child because there was no connection to any of the child's schemes and it could not be assimilated. An interplay between assimilation and accommodation of the schemes might bring about modifications that could make the situation or information that was once unproblematic now bring about a sense of dis-equilibrium in the child. This sense of dis-equilibrium could lead to further accommodation and assimilation, bringing about the development of a new scheme or a modification of the scheme and to a re-equilibration.

Piaget focused on concepts related to "natural" logic and basic reasoning processes, such as classification, seriation, and conservation, and on universals in cognitive learning such as object, space, time, causality, number, chance, and motion. He never specifically explored children's learning of mathematical notations. However, following Ferreiro, I will argue that Piaget's theory is extremely relevant to the study of this topic. This inquiry presents an interesting challenge of epistemological relevance if we consider the importance of trying to consider Piaget's theory in a domain that Piaget did not originally explore (Ferreiro, 1996b, 1997). Addressing this challenge is possible only if we consider Piaget's theory, not as a closed group of truths about the genesis of logical thought, of the concepts of space, time, causality, and mathematical and elementary physics notions, but as a general theory about the processes of cognitive learning, developed in specific domains but potentially able to explain the construction processes in other domains. As Ferreiro argues in several places (see, for example, 1996b, 1997), the fact that Piaget did not explore and study the learning of social knowledge and notation systems does not mean that the Piagetian paradigm cannot be used to explain cognitive development in these areas. In spite of the fact that the construction processes of social, cultural knowledge were not really thematized by Piaget, the essentials of his theory enable us to deal with them. As Ferreiro argues:

> Piaget's theory has a great heuristic value in the case of research concerning the psychogenesis of socio-cultural objects and in understanding [the] transformation [of sociocultural objects] into objects of knowledge. (1996a, p. 131)

Making the case for one aspect of sociocultural knowledge, literacy, Ferreiro argues that the fact that Piaget never focused his work on literacy as such does not mean that his theory is not relevant to the study of literacy development (Ferreiro, 1985). The same could be said about mathematical notations. Piaget's theory is relevant to the study of mathematical notations precisely because of the role that it assigns to the learner. In his theory, the learner is an active, knowing subject who through his/her inventions appropriates a cultural object such as notational systems. The learner that Piaget described is a knowing subject who develops knowledge, an active subject who tries to understand the world that surrounds him/her. A subject who learns through his/her own actions on the objects in the world and who constructs his/her categories of thought at the same time that s/he organizes his/her world (Ferreiro & Teberosky, 1979). The learner that Piaget described does not appropriate sociocultural knowledge by copying reality or information transmitted to him/her. The learner engages in an active process of invention of those objects of thought.

References

Aaboe, A. (1964). *Episodes from the early history of mathematics.* New York: L. W. Singer.

Alvarado, M. (2002). *La construcción del sistema gráfico numérico en los momentos iniciales de la adquisición del sistema gráfico alfabético* [The construction of the numerical graphical system in the initial moments of the acquisition of the alphabetic graphic system]. Unpublished doctoral dissertation. Mexico: Departamento de Investigaciones Educativas, CINVESTAV, IPN.

Alvarado, M., & Ferreiro, E. (2000). El análisis de nombres de números de dos dígitos en niños de 4 y 5 años [The analysis of names of two-digit numbers in 4- and 5-year-old children]. *Lectura y Vida: Revista Latinoamericana de Lectura, 21*(1), 6–17.

Ball, D. (1993). With an eye on the mathematical horizon: Dilemmas of teaching elementary school mathematics. *The Elementary School Journal, 93*(4), 373–397.

Bamberger, J. (1988). Les structurations cognitives de l'appréhension et de la notation de rythmes simples [Cognition structuring in the understanding and notation of symple rhythms]. In H. Sinclair (Ed.), *La production de notations chez le jeune enfant: Langage, nombre, rythmes et mélodies* (pp. 99–128). Paris: Presses Universitaires de France.

Bamberger, J. (1990). The laboratory for making things: Developing multiple representations of knowledge. In D. A. Schön (Ed.), *The reflective turn* (pp. 37–62). New York: Teachers College Press.

Bamberger, J. (1991). *The mind behind the musical ear: How children develop musical intelligence.* Cambridge, MA: Harvard University Press.

Bamberger, J., & Ziporyn, E. (1992). Getting it wrong. *The World of Music, 34*(3), 22–56.

Bednarz, N., & Janvier, B. (1982). The understanding of numeration in primary school. *Educational Studies in Mathematics, 13*, 33–57.

Bergeron, J. C., Herscovics, N., & Sinclair, H. (1992). Contribution à la genèse du nombre [Contribution toward the origin of number]. *Archives de Psychologie, 60*, 147–170.

Brito-Lima, A. P., & da Rocha Falcão, J. T. (1997). Early development of algebraic representation among 6–13-year-old children: The importance of didactic contract. In *Proceedings of the XXI International Conference on Psychology of Mathematics Education.* Lahti, Finland.

Brizuela, B. M. (2001). *Children's ideas about the written number system.* Unpublished doctoral dissertation, Harvard University Graduate School of Education, Cambridge, MA.

Brizuela, B. M., Carraher, D., & Schliemann, A. D. (2000). *Mathematical notation to support and further reasoning ("to help me think of something").* Paper presented as part of the research symposium "Research on Algebra in the Elementary Years" at the National Council of Teachers of Mathematics Research Presession, Chicago.

Cajori, F. (1928). *A history of mathematical notations* (Vol. 1). La Salle, IL: Open Court.

Cajori, F. (1929). *A history of mathematical notations* (Vol. 2). Chicago: Open Court.

Carpenter, T. P., Ansell, E., Franke, M. L., Fennema, E., & Weisbeck, L. (1993). Models of problem solving: A study of kindergarten children's problem-solving processes. *Journal for Research in Mathematics Education, 24*(5), 428–441.

Carraher, D. W., Brizuela, B. M., & Earnest, D. (2001). The reification of additive differences in early algebra. In H. Chick, K. Stacey, J. Vincent, & J. Vincent (Eds.), *The future of the teaching and learning of algebra: Proceedings of the 12th ICMI Study Conference* (Vol. 1, pp. 163–170). University of Melbourne, Australia.

Carraher, D. W., Brizuela, B. M., & Schliemann, A. D. (2000). Bringing out the algebraic character of arithmetic: Instantiating variables in addition and subtraction. In T. Nakahara & M. Koyama (Eds.), *Proceedings of the 24th conference of the International Group for the PME* (Vol. 2, pp. 145–152). Hiroshima, Japan: Hiroshima University.

Carraher, D. W., Schliemann, A. D., & Brizuela, B. M. (1999). *Reading algebraic meaning into the mathematics of young children.* Paper presented at a symposium at the annual meeting of the American Educational Research Association, Montreal, Canada.

Carraher, D. W., Schliemann, A. D., & Brizuela, B. M. (2001). Can young students operate on unknowns? In M. van der Heuvel-Panhuizen (Ed.), *Proceedings of the 25th conference of the International Group for the PME* (Vol. 1, pp. 130–140). Utrecht, The Netherlands: Freudenthal Institute.

Cobb, P. (1995). Cultural tools and mathematical learning: A case study. *Journal for Research in Mathematics Education, 26,* 362–385.

Cobb, P. (2000). From representations to symbolizing: Introductory comments on semiotics and mathematical learning. In P. Cobb, E. Yackel, & K. McClain (Eds.), *Symbolizing and communicating in mathematics classrooms: Perspectives on discourse, tools, and instructional design* (pp. 17–36). Mahwah, NJ: Lawrence Erlbaum.

Cobb, P., & Wheatly, G. (1988). Children's initial understandings of ten. *Focus on Learning Problems in Mathematics, 10*(3), 1–28.

Cobb, P., Yackel, E., & McClain, K. (Eds.) (2000). *Symbolizing and communicating in mathematics classrooms. Perspectives on discourse, tools, and instructional design.* Mahwah, NJ: Lawrence Erlbaum.

Confrey, J. (1991). Learning to listen: A student's understanding of powers of ten. In E. von Glasersfeld (Ed.), *Radical constructivism in mathematics education* (pp. 111–138). Dordrecht, The Netherlands: Kluwer Academic Press.

Confrey, J. (1994). Splitting, similarity, and rate of change: A new approach to multiplication and exponential functions. In G. Harel & J. Confrey (Eds.), *The development of multiplicative reasoning in the learning of mathematics* (pp. 291–330). Albany: State University of New York Press.

Confrey, J., & Smith, E. (1995). Splitting, covariation, and their role in the development of exponential functions. *Journal for Research in Mathematics Education, 26*(1), 66–86.

Cuoco, A. A., & Curcio, F. R. (Eds.). (2001). *The roles of representation in school mathematics: NCTM 2001 Yearbook.* Reston, VA: NCTM.

Davydov, V. (Ed.) (1991). *Soviet studies in mathematics education, Vol. 6: Psychological abilities of primary school children in learning mathematics.* Reston, VA: NCTM.

Dehaene, S. (1997). *The number sense: How the mind creates mathematics.* New York: Oxford University Press.

diSessa, A., Hammer, D., Sherin, B., & Kolpakowski, T. (1991). Inventing graphing: Representational expertise in children. *Journal of Mathematical Behavior, 10*, 117–160.

Duckworth, E. (1996). *The having of wonderful ideas and other essays on teaching and learning* (2nd ed.). New York: Teachers College Press.

Empson, S. B. (2002). Organizing diversity in early fraction thinking. In B. Litwiller (Ed.), *Making sense of fractions, ratios, and proportions: 2002 Yearbook* (pp. 29–40). Reston, VA: National Council of Teachers of Mathematics.

Feldman, D. H. (1994). *Beyond universals in cognitive development.* Norwood, NJ: Ablex.

Ferreiro, E. (1985). Literacy development: A psychogenetic perspective. In D. R. Olson, N. Torrance, & A. Hildyard (Eds.), *Literacy, language, and learning. The consequences of reading and writing* (pp. 217–228). New York: Cambridge University Press.

Ferreiro, E. (1986a). The interplay between information and assimilation in beginning literacy. In W. T. Teale & E. Sulzby (Eds.), *Emergent literacy: Writing and reading* (pp. 15–49). Norwood, NJ: Ablex.

Ferreiro, E. (1986b). Los procesos constructivos de apropiación de la escritura [The construction processes in the appropriation of writing]. In E. Ferreiro & M. Gomez Palacio (Eds.), *Nuevas perspectivas sobre los procesos de lectura y escritura* (8th ed., pp. 128–154). Buenos Aires: Siglo Veintiuno Editores.

Ferreiro, E. (1988). L'écriture avant la lettre [Writing before letters]. In H. Sinclair (Ed.), *La production de notations chez le jeune enfant* (pp. 17–70). Paris: Presses Universitaires de France.

Ferreiro, E. (1991). Psychological and epistemological problems on written representation of language. In M. Carretero, M. Pope, R.-J. Simons, & J. I. Pozo (Eds.), *Learning and instruction: European research in an international context* (Vol. 3, pp. 157–173). New York: Pergamon Press.

Ferreiro, E. (1996a). The acquisition of cultural objects: The case of written language. *Prospects, 26*(1), 131–140.

Ferreiro, E. (1996b). Aplicar, replicar, recrear: Acerca de las dificultades inherentes a la incorporación de nuevos objetos al cuerpo teórico de la teoría de Piaget [To apply, to replicate, to re-create: Reflections on the difficulty of incorporating new objects into the theoretical body of Piaget's theory]. *Substratum, 8*(8–9), 175–185.

Ferreiro, E. (1997). L'enfant après Piaget: Un partenaire intellectuel pour l'adulte [The child after Piaget: An intellectual partner for the adult]. *Psychologie Française, 42*(1), 69–76.

Ferreiro, E., Pontecorvo, C., Ribeiro Moreira, N., & García Hidalgo, I. (1996). *Caperucita Roja aprende a escribir* [Little Red Riding Hood learns how to write]. Barcelona: Gedisa.

Ferreiro, E., Pontecorvo, C., & Zucchermaglio, C. (1996). PIZZA or PIZA? How children interpret the doubling of letters in writing. In C. Pontecorvo, M. Orsolini, B. Burge, & L. B. Resnick (Eds.), *Children's early text construction* (pp. 145–163). Mahwah, NJ: Lawrence Erlbaum.

Ferreiro, E., & Teberosky, A. (1979). *Los sistemas de escritura en el desarrollo del niño* [Literacy before schooling]. Buenos Aires: Siglo Veintiuno Editores.

Ferreiro, E., & Zucchermaglio, C. (1996). Children's use of punctuation marks: The case of quoted speech. In C. Pontercorvo, M. Orsolini, B. Burge, & L. B. Resnick (Eds.), *Children's early text construction* (pp. 177–205). Mahwah, NJ: Lawrence Erlbaum.

Fraisse, P., & Piaget, J. (Eds.). (1969). *Experimental psychology: Its scope and method* (T. Surridge, Trans.). New York: Basic Books.

Freeman, N. (1993). Drawing: Public instruments of representation. In C. Pratt & A. F. Garton (Eds.), *Systems of representation in children* (pp. 113–132). New York: John Wiley & Sons.

Fuson, K. (1986). Roles of representation and verbalization in the teaching of multi-digit addition and subtraction. *European journal of psychology of education, 1,* 35–56.

Fuson, K. (1988). *Children's counting and concepts of number.* New York: Springer-Verlag.

García-Milà, M., Teberosky, A., & Martí, E. (2000). Anotar para resolver una tarea de localización y memoria [Making notations to solve a location and memory task]. *Infancia y Aprendizaje, 90,* 51–70.

Goldin, G. (1998). Representational systems, learning, and problem solving in mathematics. *Journal of Mathematical Behavior, 17*(2), 137–165.

Goldin, G., & Shteingold, N. (2001). Systems of representations and the development of mathematical concepts. In A. A. Cuoco & F. R. Curcio (Eds.), *The roles of representation in school mathematics: NCTM 2001 Yearbook* (pp. 1–23). Reston, VA: National Council of Teachers of Mathematics.

Gravemeijer, K., Lehrer, R., van Oers, B., & Verschaffel, L. (Eds.) (2002). *Symbolizing, modeling, and tool use in mathematics education.* Dordrecht, The Netherlands: Kluwer Academic.

Greenberg, J. H. (1978). Generalizations about numeral systems. In J. H. Greenberg (Ed.), *Universals of human language: Volume 3, Word structure* (pp. 249–295). Stanford, CA: Stanford University Press.

Gruber, H., & Vonèche, J. (Eds.) (1977). *The essential Piaget*. New York: Basic Books.

Haas, W. (1996). Sobre la escritura de los números [On the writing of numbers]. In N. Catach (Ed.), *Hacia una teoría de la lengua escrita* (pp. 257–270). Barcelona: Gedisa.

Hiebert, J., Carpenter, T. P., Fennema, E., Fuson, K., Human, P., Murray, H., et al. (1996). Problem solving as a basis for reform in curriculum and instruction: The case of mathematics. *Educational Researcher, 25*(4), 12–21.

Hughes, M. (1986). *Children and number*. Cambridge, MA: Blackwell.

Ifrah, G. (1985). *From one to zero: A universal history of numbers* (L. Bair, Trans.). New York: Viking Penguin. (Original work published 1981)

Inhelder, B., Sinclair, H., & Bovet, M. (1974). *Learning and the development of cognition* (S. Wedgwood, Trans.). Cambridge, MA: Harvard University Press.

Kamii, C. (1985). *Young children reinvent arithmetic: Implications of Piaget's theory*. New York: Teachers College Press.

Kamii, C. (1989). *Young children continue to reinvent arithmetic—2nd grade: Implications of Piaget's theory*. New York: Teachers College Press.

Kamii, C. (2000). *Young children reinvent arithmetic: Implications of Piaget's theory* (2nd ed.). New York: Teachers College Press.

Kamii, M. (1980). *Place value: Children's efforts to find a correspondence between digits and numbers of objects*. Paper presented at the Tenth Annual Symposium of the Jean Piaget Society, Philadelphia.

Kamii, M. (1982). *Children's graphical representation of numerical concepts: A developmental study*. Unpublished doctoral dissertation. Cambridge, MA: Harvard University Graduate School of Education.

Kaput, J. (1991). Notations and representations as mediators of constructive processes. In E. von Glasersfeld (Ed.), *Radical constructivism in mathematics education* (pp. 53–74). Dordrecht, The Netherlands: Kluwer Academic.

Kaput, J. (1995). *Transforming algebra from an engine of inequity to an engine of mathematical power by "algebrafying" the K–12 curriculum*. Paper presented at the annual meeting of the National Council of Teachers of Mathematics.

Karmiloff-Smith, A., & Inhelder, B. (1975). If you want to get ahead, get a theory. *Cognition, 3*, 192–212.

Kilpatrick, J. (1985). Doing mathematics without understanding: A commentary on Higbee and Kunihira. *Educational Psychologist, 20*(2), 65–68.

Lampert, M. (1989). Choosing and using mathematical tools in classroom discourse. In J. Brophy (Ed.), *Advances in Research on Teaching, 1*, 223–264.

Lee, K., & Karmiloff-Smith, A. (1996). The development of external symbol systems: The child as a notator. In R. Gelman & T. Kit-Fong Au (Eds.), *Perceptual and cognitive development: Handbook of perception and cognition* (2nd ed.) (pp. 185–211). San Diego, CA: Academic Press.

Lehrer, R., & Schauble, L. (2000). Developing model-based reasoning in mathematics and science. *Journal of Applied Developmental Psychology, 21*(1), 39–48.

Lehrer, R., & Schauble, L. (Eds.) (2002). *Investigating real data in the classroom*. New York, NY: Teachers College Press.

Lehrer, R., Schauble, L., Carpenter, S., & Penner, D. E. (2000). The inter-related development of inscriptions and conceptual understanding. In P. Cobb, E. Yackel, & K. McClain (Eds.), *Symbolizing and communicating in mathematics classrooms: Perspectives on discourse, tools, and instructional design* (pp. 325–360). Mahwah, NJ: Lawrence Erlbaum.

Leinhardt, G., Zaslavsky, O., & Stein, M. K. (1990). Functions, graphs, and graphing: Tasks, learning, and teaching. *Review of Educational Research, 60*(1), 1–64.

Lerner, D. (1994). *La matemática en la escuela: Aquí y ahora* [Mathematics in school: Here and now]. Buenos Aires: Paidós.

Lerner, D., & Sadovsky, P. (1994). El sistema de numeración: Un problema didáctico [The number system: A didactical problem]. In C. Parra & I. Saiz (Eds.), *Didáctica de matemáticas: Aportes y reflexiones* (pp. 93–184). Buenos Aires: Paidós.

Litwiller, B. (Ed.) (2002). *Making sense of fractions, ratios, and proportions: 2002 Yearbook*. Reston, VA: National Council of Teachers of Mathematics.

Martí, E., & Pozo, J. I. (2000). Más allá de las representaciones mentales: La adquisición de los sistemas externos de representación [Beyond mental representations: The acquisition of external systems of representation]. *Infancia y Aprendizaje, 90*, 11–30.

Meira, L. (2002). Mathematical representations as systems of notations-in-use. In K. Gravemeijer, R. Lehrer, B. van Oers, & L. Verschaffel, L. (Eds.), *Symbolizing, modeling, and tool use in mathematics education* (pp. 87–103). Dordrecht, The Netherlands: Kluwer Academic.

National Council of Teachers of Mathematics (NCTM). (2000). *Principles and standards for school mathematics*. Reston, VA: Author.

Nemirovsky, R. (1994). On ways of symbolizing: The case of Laura and the velocity sign. *Journal of Mathematical Behavior, 13*, 389–422.

Nemirovsky, R., Tierney, C., & Wright, T. (1998). Body motion and graphing. *Cognition and Instruction, 16*(2), 119–172.

Neugebauer, O. (1945). The history of ancient astronomy. *Journal of Near Eastern Studies, 4*(1), 2–38.

Neugebauer, O. (1962). *The exact sciences in antiquity*. New York: Harper Torchbooks.

Nunes, T., & Bryant, P. (1996). *Children doing mathematics*. Cambridge, MA: Blackwell.

Olson, D. (1994). *The world on paper*. New York: Cambridge University Press.

Parkes, M. B. (1978). Medieval punctuation, or pause and effect. In J. J. Murphy (Ed.), *Medieval eloquence* (pp. 127–142). Berkeley: University of California Press.

Parkes, M. B. (1992). *Pause and effect: An introduction to the history of punctuation in the West*. Hants, United Kingdom: Scolar Press.

Piaget, J. (1952). *The origins of intelligence in children* (M. Cook, Trans.). New York: International Universities Press. (Original work published 1936)

Piaget, J. (1969). *El nacimiento de la inteligencia en el niño* [The origins of intelligence in children] (L. Fernandez Cancela, Trans.). Madrid: Aguilar. (Original work published 1936)

Piaget, J. (1969). *The mechanisms of perception* (G. N. Seagrim, Trans.). New York: Basic Books. (Original work published 1961)

Piaget, J. (1970). Piaget's theory. In P. H. Mussen (Ed.), *Carmichael's manual of child psychology* (3rd. ed., pp. 703–732). New York: John Wiley & Sons.

Piaget, J. (1972). *Genetic epistemology* (E. Duckworth, Trans.). New York: Columbia University Press.

Piaget, J. (1973). *To understand is to invent* (G.-A. Roberts, Trans.). New York: Grossman.

Piaget, J. (1976). *The child's conception of the world* (J. & A. Tomlinson, Trans.). Totowa, NJ: Littlefield, Adams. (Original work published 1926)

Piaget, J. (1976). *The grasp of consciousness: Action and concept in the young child* (S. Wedgwood, Trans.). Cambridge, MA: Harvard University Press. (Original work published 1974)

Piaget, J. (1977). *La naissance de l'intelligence chez l'enfant* [The origins of intelligence in children] (9th. ed.) (M. Cook, Trans.). Paris: Delachaux et Niestlé. (Original work published 1936)

Piaget, J., & García, R. (1982). *Psicogénesis e historia de la ciencia* [Psychogenesis and the history of science]. México: Siglo Veintiuno Editores.

Piaget, J., & Inhelder, B. (1971). *Mental imagery in the child* (P. A. Chilton, Trans.). New York: Basic Books. (Original work published 1966)

Piaget, J., & Inhelder, B. (1973). *Memory and intelligence* (A. J. Pomerans, Trans.). New York: Basic Books. (Original work published 1968)

Quinteros, G. (1997). *El uso y función de las letras en el período pre-alfabético* [The use and role of letters in the pre-alphabetic period]. México: DIE/CINVESTAV (Thesis no. 27).

Resnick, L. B. (1983). A developmental theory of number understanding. In H. P. Ginsburg (Ed.), *The development of mathematical thinking* (pp. 109–151). New York: Academic Press.

Ross, S. H. (1986). *The development of children's place-value numeration concepts in grades two through five* (ERIC Document Reproduction Service ED273482)

Roth, W.-M. (2001). Gestures: Their role in teaching and learning. *Review of Educational Research, 71*(3), 365–392.

Sastre, G., & Moreno, M. (1976). Représentation graphique de la quantité [Graphic representation of quantity]. *Bulletin de Psychologie, 30,* 355–366.

Scheuer, N., Sinclair, A., Merlo de Rivas, S., & Tièche Christinat, C. (2000). Cuando ciento setenta y uno se escribe 10071: Niños de 5 a 8 años produciendo numerales [When one hundred seventy-one is written 10071: Children 5 to 8 years old producing numerals]. *Infancia y Aprendizaje, 90,* 31–50.

Schifter, D. (1998). *Developing operation sense as a foundation for algebra I.* Unpublished manuscript.

Schliemann, A. D., Carraher, D. W., & Brizuela, B. M. (2001). When tables become function tables. In M. van der H.-P. (Ed.), *Proceedings of the 25th conference of the International Group for the PME* (Vol. 4, pp. 145–152). Utrecht, The Netherlands: Freudenthal Institute.

Schliemann, A. D., Carraher, D. W., Pendexter, W., & Brizuela, B. (1998). *Solving algebra problems before algebra instruction.* Paper presented at the Second Early Algebra Meeting, Tufts University/UMass-Dartmouth.

Schwartz, J. (1988). Intensive quantities and referent transforming arithmetic operations. In J. Hiebert & M. Behr (Eds.), *Number concepts and operations in the middle grades* (Vol. 2, pp. 41–52). Reston, VA: LEA & National Council of Teachers of Mathematics.

Schwartz, J. (1996). *Semantic aspects of quantity.* Unpublished manuscript. Cambridge, MA: MIT and Harvard Graduate School of Education.

Schwartz, J., & Yerushalmy, M. (1995). On the need for a bridging language for mathematical modeling. *For the Learning of Mathematics, 15*(2), 29–35.

Sellke, D. H., Behr, M. J., & Voelker, A. M. (1991). Using data tables to represent and solve multiplicative story problems. *Journal for Research in Mathematics Education, 22*(1), 30–38.

Sharp, J. M., Garofalo, J., & Adams, B. (2002). Children's development of meaningful fraction algorithms: A kid's cookies and a puppy's hills. In B. Litwiller (Ed.), *Making sense of fractions, ratios, and proportions: 2002 yearbook* (pp. 18–28). Reston, VA: National Council of Teachers of Mathematics.

Simon, M., & Stimpson, V. C. (1988). Developing algebraic representation using diagrams. In A. F. Coxford & A. P. Shulte (Eds.), *The ideas of algebra, K–12: 1988 yearbook* (pp. 136–141). Reston, VA: National Council of Teachers of Mathematics.

Sinclair, A. (1988). La notation numérique chez l'enfant [Numerical notation in children]. In H. Sinclair (Ed.), *La production de notation chez le jeune enfant* (pp. 71–97). Paris: Presses Universitaires de France.

Sinclair, A., & Scheuer, N. (1993). Understanding the written number system: 6-year-olds in Argentina and Switzerland. *Educational Studies in Mathematics, 24,* 199–221.

Sinclair, A., & Sinclair, H. (1984). Preschool children's interpretation of written numbers. *Human Learning, 3,* 173–184.

Sinclair, H. (1982). *Children's ideas about written words and written numbers.* Division for Study and Research in Education Working Paper 14. Cambridge: Massachusetts Institute of Technology.

Smith, J. P. (2002). The development of students' knowledge of fractions and ratios. In B. Litwiller (Ed.), *Making sense of fractions, ratios, and proportions: 2002 yearbook* (pp. 3–17). Reston, VA: National Council of Teachers of Mathematics.

Steffe, L., & Cobb, P. (1988). *Construction of arithmetical meanings and strategies.* New York: Springer-Verlag.

Streefland, L. (1985). Search for the roots of ratio: Some thoughts on the long term learning process (towards . . . a theory). Part II. The outline of the long term learning process. *Educational Studies in Mathematics, 16,* 75–94.

Struik, D. J. (1987). *A concise history of mathematics* (4th ed.). New York: Dover.

Tierney, C., & Nemirovsky, R. (1995). *Children's graphing of changing situations.* Paper presented at the annual meeting of the AERA, San Francisco.

Tolchinsky, L. (1993). *Aprendizaje del lenguaje escrito* [Learning of written language]. Barcelona: Anthropos.

Tolchinsky, L., & Karmiloff-Smith, A. (1992). Children's understanding of notations as domains of knowledge versus referential-communicative tools. *Cognitive Development, 7,* 287–300.

Treitler, L. (1982). The early history of music writing in the West. *Journal of the American Musicological Society, 35*(2), 237–279.

Vergnaud, G. (1985). Concepts et schemes dans une theorie operatoire de la representation [Concepts and schemes in an operatory theory of representation]. *Psychologie Française, 30*(3–4), 245–252.

Vergnaud, G. (1988). Multiplicative structures. In J. Hiebert & M. Behr (Eds.), *Number and operations in the middle grades* (pp. 141–161). Hillsdale, NJ: LEA/National Council of Teachers of Mathematics.

Vygotsky, L. S. (1978). *Mind in society. The development of higher psychological processes.* Cambridge, MA: Harvard University Press.

Vygotsky, L. S. (1986). *Thought and language.* Cambridge, MA: MIT Press.

Willis, G. B., & Fuson, K. C. (1988). Teaching children to use schematic drawings to solve addition and subtraction word problems. *Journal of Educational Psychology, 80*(2), 192–201.

Index

About the Author

Bárbara M. Brizuela is an assistant professor of education at Tufts University. She is a former early childhood and elementary school teacher who completed her university studies in her home country, Argentina. She completed her graduate studies in the United States, at Tufts University and Harvard Graduate School of Education. She has received a Spencer Foundation Research Training Grant and has published in journals such as the *American Educational Research Journal, For the Learning of Mathematics,* and the *Journal of Mathematical Behavior.* Her work has been published in English, Spanish, and Portuguese. Her focus of research is in cognitive development and mathematics education. She currently works with children and teachers in public schools in the Boston area.